C000273120

Manningham

Character and diversity in a Bradford suburb

Manningham

Character and diversity in a Bradford suburb

Simon Taylor and Kathryn Gibson

'Bradford is the best city in the world
and England is the best country in the world ...
Manningham is the best place in Bradford.'

Khadam Hussain – Chairperson, Victor Street Mosque

ENGLISH HERITAGE

Front cover
Manningham and Manningham Mills looking west. Manningham is a place of contrasts and diversity as this view and this book seek to demonstrate. Historic industrial, residential and institutional zones and buildings exist in close proximity and various different communities have always lived side by side in, and been nurtured by, this solid, stone-built Victorian suburb.
[DP072458]

Inside front cover
Detail from Thomas Dixon's Map of the Borough of Bradford, surveyed in 1844–6.
[Reproduced by permission of Bradford Libraries, Archives and Information Service, DP098005]

Frontispiece
Aerial view of Lister Park and the Edmund Cartwright Memorial Hall, Manningham.
[NMR/20850/045]

Acknowledgements
Detail from plinth of S C Lister's statue in Lister Park.
[DP071608]

Back cover
The entrance to the former offices of Manningham Mills which faced eastwards onto Heaton Road and the middle-class houses between the Mills and Lister Park.
[DP071981]

Published by English Heritage, Kemble Drive, Swindon SN2 2GZ
www.english-heritage.org.uk
English Heritage is the Government's statutory adviser on all aspects of the historic environment.

© English Heritage 2010

Images (except as otherwise shown) © English Heritage, © English Heritage.NMR or © English Heritage.NMR Aerofilms Collection

Figures 7, 22, 76 and the map on p 107 are © Crown Copyright and database right 2010. All rights reserved. Ordnance Survey Licence number 100019088.

The *Tales and Trails of Manningham* DVD is reproduced under licence from © Connexions Humber. Film commissioned and produced on behalf of English Heritage.

First published 2010
Reprinted 2011

ISBN 978 1 84802 030 6
Product code 51475

British Library Cataloguing in Publication Data
A CIP catalogue record for this book is available from the British Library.

All rights reserved
No part of this publication may be reproduced or transmitted in any form or by any means, electronic or mechanical, including photocopying, recording, or any information storage or retrieval system, without permission in writing from the publisher.

Application for the reproduction of images should be made to the National Monuments Record. Every effort has been made to trace the copyright holders and we apologise in advance for any unintentional omissions, which we would be pleased to correct in any subsequent edition of this book.

The National Monuments Record is the public archive of English Heritage. For more information, contact NMR Enquiry and Research Services, National Monuments Record Centre, Kemble Drive, Swindon SN2 2GZ; telephone (01793) 414600.

Typeset in ITC Charter 9.25pt on 13pt

Photographs by Bob Skingle and Simon Taylor
Aerial photographs by David MacLeod
Graphics by Allan T Adams and Rachel Cross
Brought to publication by Jess Ward, Publishing, English Heritage
Edited by Susan Kelleher
Page layout by George Hammond
Printed in Belgium by DeckersSnoeck

Contents

Acknowledgements

The production of this booklet and DVD was greatly assisted by Christine Kerrin and Jon Ackroyd of the City of Bradford Metropolitan District Council; George Sheeran of the University of Bradford; Sofia Maskin and all who took part in the outreach project; and the staffs of the Local Studies section of Bradford Central Library and the West Yorkshire Archive Service, Bradford. Additional thanks are due to George Sheeran for commenting on the text. We would also like to thank Joy Leach and Bruce Barnes, Julia and Peter Reynell, and the Bradford Eesti Kodu Club for their particular help with our survey work.

We would also like to express our gratitude for the assistance and support provided by our colleagues in English Heritage. The photographs were taken by Bob Skingle and Simon Taylor, and the aerial photographs by Dave MacLeod. Allan T Adams and Rachel Cross produced the drawings and maps and John Cattell, Colum Giles, Trevor Mitchell and Adam Menuge commented on the text. The survey and research was undertaken by Allan T Adams, Naomi Archer, Allison Borden, Kate Bould, Deborah Lamb, Bob Skingle, Simon Taylor and Matthew Withey. The outreach project was managed by Helen Keighley and Trina Nielsen.

Foreword

At the height of the Industrial Revolution, Bradford was the centre of the world's worsted trade. It achieved this position through a flair for international trade, technical innovation and business acumen, combined with powerful civic pride. Once a sparsely populated outlying village, Manningham developed to become Bradford's premier Victorian suburb. But while its comfortable villas are a testament to the wealth of Bradford's leading citizens, Manningham also contains fine examples of elegant terraced housing and smaller back-to-back homes, as well as mill complexes and a wide range of public buildings. Together, these produce a patchwork of strikingly contrasting neighbourhoods.

Our built heritage provides a link to our past, but it is the lives of people that give us an immediate connection to our history. Modern Manningham is a vibrant, multicultural community, but so too was Victorian Manningham. Over the years, every social and cultural group has experienced the area in different ways, and each has left its mark. Understanding how different people feel about their surroundings brings places to life and reveals the communal values that they hold.

We are therefore pleased that in the preparation of this book it has been possible to make an innovative DVD capturing the views and memories of today's residents.

In recent decades Manningham has had a reputation as a rundown area with problems. But the acclaimed restoration of Lister Park and the landmark conversion of Lister Mills heralds a new era. Historic elements such as these help to maintain a sense of place and bind communities together. As other developments follow, it is vital that the exceptional interest and quality of Manningham's buildings, streets and open spaces is recognised and sustained. A revival of the area's fortunes will require change, just as previous generations altered what they found, building and adapting to suit their needs. Well-judged, proportionate change will enhance, not diminish, the suburb's special qualities, but defining them is an essential first step. This book provides a marvellous foundation. It considers how Manningham came into being, how contemporaries viewed it, what it means to today's residents and how its best qualities can be retained for the future.

Baroness Andrews, Chair, English Heritage

Councillor Anne Hawkesworth, City of Bradford Metropolitan District Council

1

Introduction: a Bradford suburb

High above the sprawling city that obscures a lost Yorkshire dale stands Manningham Mills, one of the most dramatic expressions of Victorian England's industrial prowess. Its famous Italianate chimney and the bulky mass of the process buildings are visible for miles, and for many people coming to Bradford they symbolise the city and its industrial past. But Manningham is, and has always been, a place of contrasts and diversity and provides a richer, more layered insight into both Bradford's past and the specific role played by Manningham itself. Just a short distance to the north-east of Manningham Mills is the paradisal Lister Park where the Edmund Cartwright Memorial Hall, Bradford's museum and art gallery, stands. Beyond are tree-lined streets of classical and Gothic-styled villas of yellow stone, the former homes of Bradford's professional and mercantile elite. To the south and west stretches a sea of good-quality terraced houses, many of them back-to-backs which, contrary to the stereotypical view of back-to-backs as slum dwellings, were once the homes of tradesmen and artisans, and even schoolteachers. At the centre of all is the ancient village of Manningham, the nucleus of a once rural township, now marked by the tall spire of St Paul's Church, built in 1847 when the township became part of Bradford borough. Close by is the former Bradford Children's Hospital of 1890 with its distinctive circular ward tower and the garden-like retreat of the Bradford Tradesmen's Homes (built 1867–70 and 1878) – less well-known than Titus Salt's model village of Saltaire (built 1853–76), but equally expressive of his philanthropic zeal. As part of a mushrooming Victorian city, Manningham did indeed also have its industrialised zones. Both to the east and to the south the valley of the Bradford Beck attracted factory development, including huge worsted mills and dye works at Brown Royd and Thornton Road. Here and there, in marked contrast, late 18th and early 19th-century cottage rows speak of an earlier, smaller-scale domestic textile industry that had largely evaporated by the middle of the 19th century.

These buildings, varied in function and scale, tell a story of suburb building which is in some ways common to many English towns and cities, but which has a distinctive stamp of its own. Across the country unprecedented population growth and the deterioration of urban environments persuaded many better-off 19th-century town dwellers to opt for a suburban residence. Typically it was the wealthiest who moved first, but others soon followed,

Figure 1
Statue of Samuel Cunliffe Lister erected in 1875 at the southern entrance to Lister Park.
[DP071612]

frequently ousting those who had gone before and moved on to more exclusive areas, often profiting from the sale of their land for denser housing developments. In Manningham, from the 1830s, housing of different patterns and for widely differing social groups grew up more or less simultaneously, some of it alongside new industrial developments. At first these varied developments were suburban islands, isolated from one another by green fields, but as Manningham grew they met to produce a patchwork of districts of contrasting social composition and architectural form.

Manningham's varying character can be traced in part to the actions of a few wealthy individuals and in part to the collective – often mutual – effort of many lesser citizens. The two most prominent Bradfordian personalities of the 19th century were Samuel Cunliffe Lister (1815–1906) (Fig 1) and Titus Salt (1803–76) (Fig 2), both giants of the textile industry. The former built Manningham Mills (now known as Lister Mills), and endowed Bradford with Lister Park and the Edmund Cartwright Memorial Hall. The latter paid for the Bradford Tradesmen's Homes and was the driving force within the Bradford Freehold Land Society which bought and laid out Girlington, in the west of Manningham township, in an attempt to help working men buy their own homes and thereby gain the vote. Private capital, building clubs and societies, and co-operative societies also played their part, building distinctive suburban districts in response to the particular needs of different economic groups, while competing religious faiths and sects punctuated the landscape with a fine stock of churches, chapels and synagogues. At its height Manningham was regarded as Bradford's premier residential suburb. It was the 'best end of town' and a byword for status, style and exclusivity – tree-lined and cosmopolitan in parts and also remote and aloof from the bustling business world of central Bradford.

Manningham gained prominence in the second half of the 19th century when Bradford mushroomed as the world centre for the production of both worsted and mixed-fibre 'Orleans' cloth (the former was a cloth made from the long staple of the fleece which was generally lighter and finer than woollen cloths with a smooth rather than felted finish and visible weave, the latter had a cotton warp and a woollen weft which was often alpaca or mohair). However, textiles had played an important role in the economy of the Bradford area since at least the 17th century and the West Riding of Yorkshire had been one of the country's principal producers of woollen cloth for some time, thanks

Figure 2
Statue of Sir Titus Salt at the northern end of Lister Park. Originally located outside Bradford Town Hall, the statue was moved to its present location, facing towards Saltaire, in 1896.
[DP071838]

to the efforts of huge numbers of independent clothiers. Such men made up the cloth pieces, the standard-sized units in which cloth was sold, in their homes using their own labour and that of their family and often supplemented their income by working a small farm. From the late 17th century, the Bradford area combined woollen cloth production with the manufacture of worsted cloth with such colourful names as shalloons, calamancoes and camblets, now almost forgotten. Worsted production was the province of clothiers who acted as co-ordinators, supplying the materials to make cloth to scattered outworkers, who variously combed (the all-important process, peculiar to the worsted industry, of removing the short wool fibres from the long staple and combing it straight), spun, and wove in their homes using their own machinery. The clothiers would sell the finished pieces in the local cloth halls or direct to merchants.

Bradford's transformation from small Pennine town to industrial and commercial powerhouse occurred relatively late compared to neighbouring West Riding towns. Huddersfield, Halifax and Leeds, for example, were already booming commercially by the early 18th century, but Bradford's rise had faltered towards the end of the 17th century and the town was slow to recover. By the second half of the 18th century, however, the town's trade and growth were sufficient to prompt the building of the Bradford Canal, which opened in 1774. Over the next two or three generations the system of domestic outworking was overtaken by the factory system with its multi-storey mills and its concentrated and increasingly urbanised labour force. By 1810 at least six textile mills had been built in Bradford but the town had still not expanded much beyond its boundaries of 1700. John Johnson's map of 1802 (Fig 3) depicts a small compact town centred on a marketplace with some linear expansion north-westwards along Westgate. To the immediate south, west and north lay the outlying townships of Bowling, Great and Little Horton and Manningham respectively which, together with Bradford township stretching out to the east, would later comprise the first municipal borough of Bradford.

The building developments shown by Johnson along Westgate lay in the direction of Manningham. In little more than half a century, two-thirds of Manningham township was transformed from an area of thinly populated countryside, with a small, nucleated but church-less village roughly at its

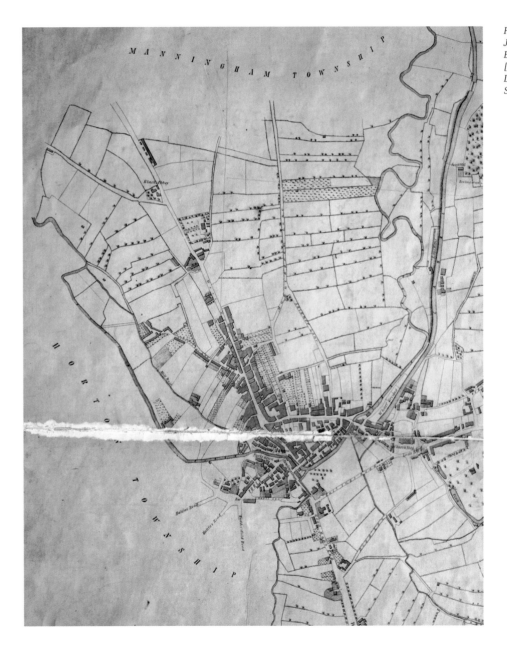

Figure 3
John Johnson's map of the township of
Bradford, 1802.
[Reproduced by permission of Bradford
Libraries, Archives and Information
Service, DP098017]

centre, into a mixed residential suburb hedged and encroached upon by industrial corridors and crowned by Manningham Mills. This growth coincided with a period when great wealth was accumulated by the fortunate and industrious few, while living standards for the remainder improved only slowly as wages gradually rose and the need for tighter regulation of the urban environment was recognised and acted upon. Manningham Lane, historically one of the main approaches to Bradford from the north, grew in stature, acquiring rows of substantial, ashlar-fronted houses and, closer to the town, larger commercial buildings that anticipated the great wool emporia of Bradford itself. Residential areas, of both high and low status, developed to its east and west boasting wide streets and solid, attractively detailed, ashlar-fronted Victorian houses (the larger ones with substantial porches, verandas and boldly panelled front doors). The majority of the houses were built of locally quarried yellow sandstone lending the area a unified appearance. However, with such a wide social range represented by the architecture, Victorian Manningham's underlying identity is less clear – to whom did it really belong? Was it one place or was it a loose agglomeration of many?

The question of identity is just as relevant when asked of Manningham today. Now an inner-city suburb of Bradford Metropolitan District, its old boundaries are blurred and its fortunes have been mixed. But Manningham is still the busy, bustling home of a series of close communities. There has been some loss of individual buildings and streets while others bear the scars of years of neglect, but many have benefited from recent investment. Manningham's elevated position and rich architectural heritage can still be enjoyed, and have the potential to underpin future prosperity. The conversion of Manningham Mills to apartments is a demonstration of faith in the area's future and looks set to trigger other conversions of redundant buildings, the retention of which is so important to the distinctive character of the place. Key developments such as these can rejuvenate areas and prompt more widespread regeneration and revival. This book charts the growth of Manningham as a place, the emergence of its identity, the day-to-day experience of the people who lived and worked there during its heyday, and the changes that the 20th century brought to it. Unravelling these strands of its history allows us to see more clearly why Manningham is important and what measures will best ensure that the historic environment continues to benefit future generations.

2

A lost landscape

Figure 4
Bradford Dale from Cutler Heights. Although not geographically part of the Yorkshire Dales, Bradford Dale stands comparison with Airedale and Nidderdale as a partly industrialised Yorkshire river valley.
[DP071799]

Figure 5
The Bradford Beck at Shipley.
[DP071771]

The historic township of Manningham occupies roughly 533.5 hectares of elevated ground to the north-west of the modern centre of Bradford (*see* Fig 7). The village of Manningham is situated close to its heart and is itself roughly 2km from the middle of Bradford. The township boundaries to the east and south follow the Bradford Beck, which rises in the Pennine hills to the west of Bradford and flows eastward into the city in a deep valley known as Bradford Dale (Fig 4) before turning northwards to join the River Aire at Shipley (Fig 5). A tributary, Chellow Dene Beck, forms part of Manningham's western boundary. Manningham township lies between the two arms of the Bradford Beck on land that slopes gently towards the south and east before falling more steeply to the valley floor. To the north-west the land continues to rise to become Cottingley Moor beyond Heaton. Today it is hard to imagine this part of the dale and the low moors as they would have been two centuries or more ago – although there are clues in the recurrence of such place names as 'Royd' which means a clearing in woods and conjures images of a densely wooded medieval landscape. Now the woods have gone and the contours of the landscape have been obscured by the sprawling growth of urban Bradford.

Manningham's origins as an administrative unit are ancient, if unremarkable, and it is thought to be one of six outlying dependencies of the manor of Bradford which are noted but not named in the Domesday Book. In 1322 the manor was seized by Edward II following his defeat of its heir, the Earl of Lancaster, who had participated in a plot to overthrow him, although this change in succession probably had little effect on life in the outlying townships. The Black Death took its toll later in the 14th century, and in 1379 just 19 adults were included in the poll tax return.[1] The Lister family, whose name is almost synonymous with that of Manningham itself, came to the township during the reign of Henry VIII when Thomas Lister, grandson of Sir William Lister of Thornton-in-Craven, married the daughter and heiress of a Bradford clothier named Richard King, and by this alliance acquired the Lister estates in Manningham.[2]

By the early 17th century there were about 30 homesteads in Manningham, 12 of them making up Manningham village, and they are depicted on a map of the township made in 1613 by Robert Saxton (Fig 6). Saxton reveals a landscape that had evolved from medieval times, divided into

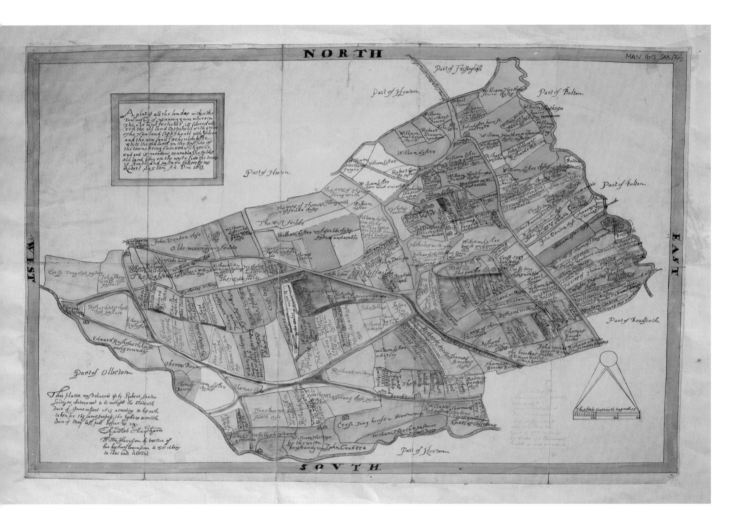

Figure 6
Robert Saxton's 1613 map of the township
of Manningham.
[Reproduced by permission of Bradford
Libraries, Archives and Information
Service, DP098003]

Figure 7
Location map showing the position of the old township of Manningham and the wider Bradford area.

Figure 8
The early 17th-century Old Manor House, Rosebery Road, after reduction and remodelling in the late 19th century.
[DP065449]

meadows, pastures, arable land, and the old 'town fields' which are named. Ownership was divided between 41 individuals with the Lister family holding large areas, especially in the north of the township. Most of the 12 houses in the village were clustered around an area called 'The garthe' – probably the village green – between modern Carlisle Road and Church Street. The main roads that Saxton shows in the township are still recognisable today – Manningham Lane, Toller Lane, Skinner Lane, Church Street, Thornton Road, Whetley Lane, Whetley Hill and the junction at Four Lane Ends. Most still serve as main thoroughfares today, and although often widened and regularised, their courses are still distinguishable from the straighter lines of many 19th-century streets. Bradford was at this time an important centre of textile production, and marketing and manufacturing would have been a major occupation in the surrounding townships including Manningham. The roads and lanes that Saxton shows would doubtless have been busy with the traffic from farms and cottages in this complex chain of production.

The only building which survives from this period stands beside what is now called Rosebery Road and is known as the Old Manor House (Fig 8),

9

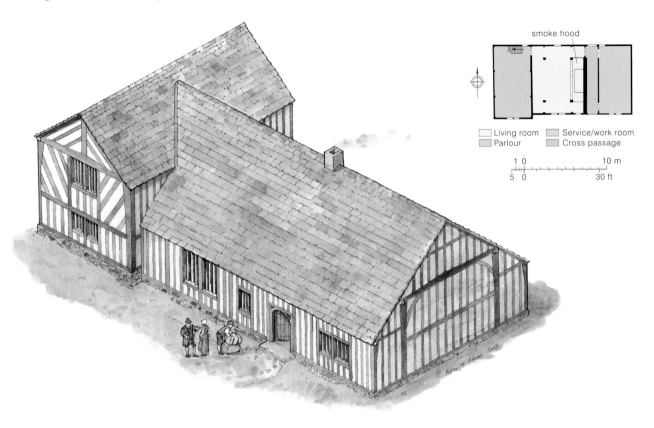

smoke hood

Living room | Service/work room
Parlour | Cross passage

1 0   10 m
5 0   30 ft

although the name is misleading because Manningham was not itself a manor. Nevertheless the house must have belonged to a wealthy yeoman, probably a farmer and clothier. Saxton's map names this part of Manningham, on the edge of the village, as 'Lilliecrofte meadowe', and according to the schedule which accompanied the map it belonged to John Denton. He held just over 10 acres (4.04ha) of land adjoining his house and a little over eight acres (3.23ha) elsewhere in the township. Originally timber-framed and boasting a double-aisled hall (something of a rarity in West Yorkshire) the house was comprehensively rebuilt in stone in the first half of the 17th century, probably in the 1620s (Fig 9). The house was modified and reduced in size in the late 19th century and what survives today is part of the hall (the general living room of the house) and a

Figure 9
Phase 1: The Old Manor House in the early 16th century when fully timber framed. It was probably the home of a yeoman clothier, his family and some servants, and would also have served as his business premises.

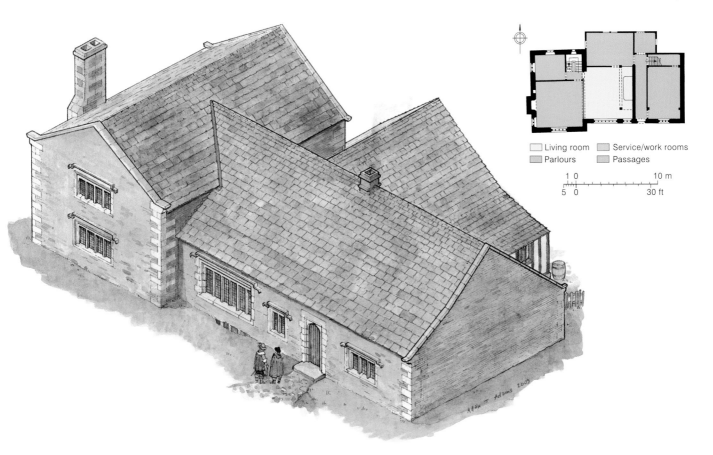

Living room   Service/work rooms
Parlours   Passages

1 0   10 m
5 0   30 ft

Phase 2: The Old Manor House was largely rebuilt in stone in the early to mid-17th century, probably in the 1620s. A new cross-wing replaced the medieval one, providing a heated parlour and heated chamber along with other rooms and a staircase. Additional service rooms were also added to the rear of the house.

two-storeyed cross-wing containing the parlour and other rooms. Now unoccupied and semi-derelict, it is the only built reminder of the Manningham that Robert Saxton observed in 1613.

In the 17th century Manningham was probably the least populous of the Bradford manor townships. When assessed for the hearth tax in 1672 only 65 houses were recorded as taxable compared to 66 in Bowling, 124 in Horton and 203 in Bradford itself. The hearth tax tells us little or nothing about the houses beyond the number of fireplaces, but this does at least give us a rough idea of their size, quality and modernity, and comparison with Bradford, where many incomes were augmented by commerce in the town, helps to highlight the difference this made. One house in Bradford, for example, had a grand total of 10 hearths and many had two or three. The

11

best-equipped house in Manningham, Thomas Lister's, had seven, while John Denton's, with five, was also clearly one of the most substantial as most of Manningham's residents, including those too poor to be taxed, benefited from just a single hearth. While one hearth does not necessarily equate to a small house, it is clear that Manningham at this date was not a particularly wealthy rural township.

And so it remained, by and large, for another century and a half. The township was tied to the wider parish through its dependence on Bradford's parish church and marketplace, and farmers ground their corn at the Bradford Soke Mills (which were in any case at Brown Royd on the township boundary to the south-west). Otherwise Manningham was reasonably autonomous,

Figure 10
The former Lister Arms, also known as the Spotted House, beside Manningham Lane. Although the present building is ostensibly a former 19th-century public house, a pub called the Green Spot had stood on the site since at least the 16th century.
[DP071982]

having its own constables and churchwardens who were appointed annually at town meetings (held, from the early 19th century, at the Old or Upper Globe Inn on Thornton Road), while Ellis Cunliffe Lister held court as Justice of the Peace at the Bench meeting of the magistrates at the Lister's Arms, later the Spotted House, beside Manningham Lane (Fig 10). From time to time new buildings were erected or existing ones modernised. Among the most notable was the Clock House (Fig 11). In origin another of Manningham's ancient homesteads and depicted on Saxton's map, it was acquired by a tanner named Thomas Crabtree in 1636 and had five hearths in 1672. Crabtree's family rebuilt it around 1700 and it was altered again by a new owner, Nathan Jowett, in about 1783: it now houses Bradford Grammar Junior School. Of particular note is the erection in about 1770 of the two-storeyed and classically styled Manningham Hall by the Listers, close to the site of the family's old homestead of Hill Top.

In 1783 Manningham's freeholders decided to enclose the old waste ground of Manningham Common where the freeholders of the township traditionally grazed their livestock.[3] The enclosure of a common usually profited only the freeholders who divided the land amongst themselves with little direct benefit to the poor – but here the freeholders were too numerous to make such a division viable. Instead it was agreed that the land would be let out for farming by a trust comprising the leading freeholders, which included 'Mr Lister' and 'Mr Jowett' (Nathan Jowett's father), and that once the income from rents, etc had met the initial cost of enclosing and improving the land, future rental income would be given over to the poor of the township. As part of the enclosure agreement 12 closes (enclosed pieces of land), at Daisy Hill were also given to the poor and it was here that both Daisy Hill Cottages (for the aged poor) and the Daisy Hill Institution (now Lynfield Mount Hospital) were built a century later.

Manningham was still the least populous of the four townships, having less than 1,000 inhabitants in 1780 compared to more than 4,500 in Bradford. By this time, however, textile manufacturing in the Bradford area was once again growing in importance. Indeed by 1780 the West Riding of Yorkshire had overtaken East Anglia as the largest worsted producing area in the country. During the 18th century, local merchants began exporting cloth not just to their traditional markets in Northern Europe but to the Mediterranean, and

Figure 11
*The Clock House, Manningham Lane. The present
house probably dates from around 1700, although it
was remodelled and altered subsequently. The name is
said to refer to a clock, the first to be brought to this
part of the country, which was formerly placed on the
south front of the house in such a way that the time
could be read by travellers on the main road to Otley.
[DP065437]*

later North America and the West Indies. The men of the trade were, on the whole, just small-scale independent businessmen but their success led to the opening of the Bradford Piece Hall at the end of Kirkgate in 1773, which provided a central exchange where domestic manufacturers could sell their goods to buyers in a secure environment. A number of piece halls were built in Yorkshire in the 18th century, an indication of the importance and sophistication of the textile industry even before the introduction of powered factories.

The year after the opening of the Piece Hall the Bradford Canal opened, enabling easier shipments of goods than the network of turnpike roads had hitherto permitted. The canal followed a course roughly parallel to that of the Bradford Beck along the eastern boundary of the township, and extended as far as Shipley and the Leeds and Liverpool Canal, then still under construction. By 1777 the Leeds and Liverpool Canal had connected Bradford with Leeds and the Aire and Calder Navigation, giving Bradford's merchants and manufacturers improved access to the port of Hull and continental markets, although the desired link with Liverpool was not completed until 1816. Worsted manufacture in Bradford was also retarded by the reluctance of its manufacturers to embrace the factory system of production, which has sometimes been attributed to the slow flow of Bradford Beck and its unsuitability for driving machinery. There were, by contrast, many worsted mills on the fast-flowing streams around Halifax, but it was only after 1800, by which time steam engines offered an alternative to water power, that Bradford began to resemble a true factory town. The first mill in Bradford is usually reckoned to be Holme Mill, in place by 1800, and by 1810 six mills had been built in the town. Even so, a large proportion of worsted yarn spinning was still undertaken by hand in domestic environments, as was all the combing and weaving. Since the powered mechanisation of both combing and weaving lagged behind that of spinning, greater numbers of combers and weavers were required to supply and keep pace with the output of the powered spinning mills.

The impact of these changes on Manningham was initially modest, as can be seen by comparing the map made in 1811 by a Bradford land surveyor named George Leather (Fig 12) with Robert Saxton's map of nearly two centuries previously (*see* Fig 6). But there are indications, nevertheless, that the early decades of the 19th century, and perhaps the latter years of the 18th century, were characterised by rapid change. The township's population had reached 1,357 inhabitants by the beginning of the 19th century and it was rising fast, nearly doubling to 2,474 by 1821. Of this total, the entry for Manningham in Edward Baines's *History, Directory & Gazetteer of the County of York* (1822) distinguishes just 39 principal residents. The occupations of some, like the 4 publicans, 2 blacksmiths and 6 grocers, would be common to villagers across much of England but others are less typical. Ellis Cunliffe Lister of Manningham Hall, Joseph Hollings of Whitley Hall and Richard Hodgson, also of Whitley, head the list of Manningham's citizens alongside Miss Sarah Jowitt of Clock House, and two others listed as 'gentlemen', suggesting that there may already have been a trend to establish genteel residences beyond the urban fringe. Two quarry owners and three stone masons point to a lively building trade – not just in Manningham but also in nearby Bradford. The three worsted manufacturers, two spinners, a woolstapler and a shuttle maker make up a substantial proportion of the trades listed although the full extent of the labour force is unreported. Even though Manningham seems to have been a less important textile producer than some neighbouring townships (at the late date of 1837 there were 10 hand looms operating in Horton for every one in Manningham) it is likely that a significant proportion of the many inhabitants *not* listed by Baines were engaged in domestic textile outworking. This shift in the balance of economic activity may be connected with the appearance, since Saxton's map, of a series of hamlets at Daisy Hill, Whetley, White Abbey and Four Lane Ends.

More certain evidence of the worsted industry's impact on Manningham comes from the piecemeal adaptation of existing buildings and the building of new cottages, probably to accommodate weavers, which are scattered around Manningham village and also nearby in Heaton. Typically, domestic textile workers' houses in the Bradford area were simple vernacular structures of rubble stone lit by two or three-light stone-mullioned windows, with doors with monolithic jambs, and roofed with heavy sandstone slates. Usually two storeys high with only one room per floor, they were built in rows, sometimes by squatters on patches of unexploited land, with communal yards or gardens. Sleeping and living accommodation was provided on the ground floor while the first floor was usually used as the workshop and perhaps sleeping quarters

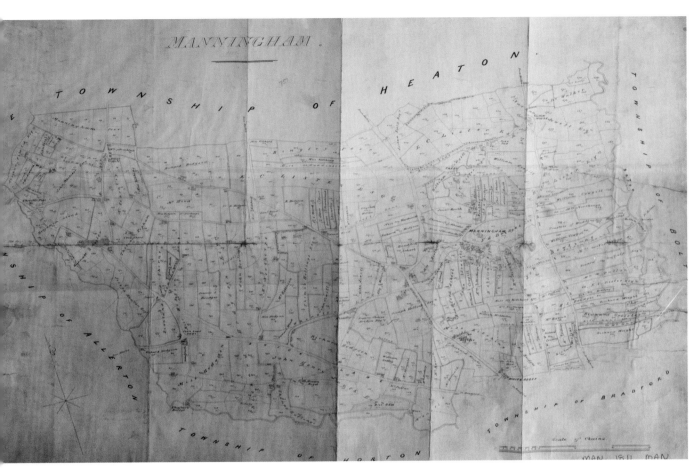

Figure 12
George Leather's 1811 map of Manningham which
accompanied a survey of the township in the same year.
[Reproduced by permission of Bradford Libraries,
Archives and Information Service, DP098013]

for children.[4] A row of three cottages, Nos. 11, 13 and 15 Skinner Lane (Fig 13), for example, were originally built as a single farmhouse which was subdivided into three dwellings in the late 18th or early 19th century. Its use for domestic manufacturing is indicated by a single first-floor taking-in doorway, now blocked (Fig 14). Nos. 30–38 Whetley Hill (Fig 15) had been opportunistically built by 1811 on an island in the middle of an early meeting of roads (Toller Lane, Church Street and Whetley Hill), creating Cross Road, and Nos. 36–48 Heaton Road, a single-phase terrace of six cottages, was also there by 1811 (Fig 16). Similar cottages further south on Heaton Road and on the north side of Church Street are slightly later, perhaps having been built in the 1820s. A little to the north in Heaton is Garden Terrace (Fig 17), a south-facing and curving row of two-storeyed cottages built beside Syke Road in about 1800. Syke Road takes its name from the stream, or syke, which once flowed above ground, feeding Heaton Reservoir, from a spring on the west side of Heaton Road. The spring, which can still be seen today pouring into a stone trough beside the road, is celebrated in the name of the former 'Fountain' public house

Figure 13 (left, above)
Nos. 11, 13 and 15 Skinner Lane. Once a single house it was divided into three dwellings for domestic textile manufacturers.
[DP065773]

Figure 14 (left, below)
The inserted taking-in door at No. 11 Skinner Lane suggests a first-floor workshop.
[DP071540]

Figure 15 (above)
Nos. 30–38 Whetley Hill were built in two phases on a small patch of land which was formerly part of a road junction. There are five cottages which share a walled and gated front yard but only a narrow verge separates them from Cross Street to the rear.
[DP071063]

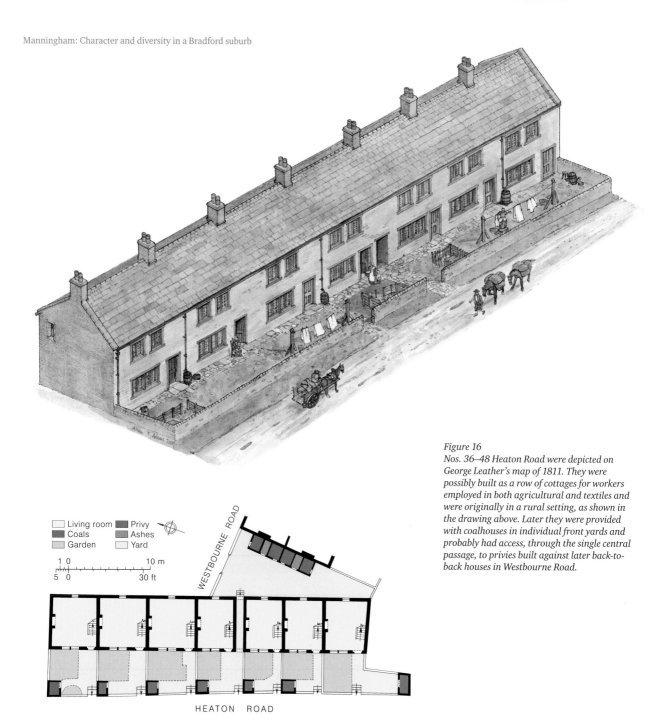

Figure 16
Nos. 36–48 Heaton Road were depicted on George Leather's map of 1811. They were possibly built as a row of cottages for workers employed in both agricultural and textiles and were originally in a rural setting, as shown in the drawing above. Later they were provided with coalhouses in individual front yards and probably had access, through the single central passage, to privies built against later back-to-back houses in Westbourne Road.

Living room   Privy
Coals   Ashes
Garden   Yard

1 0   10 m
5 0   30 ft

WESTBOURNE ROAD

HEATON ROAD

on the corner of Syke Road. It may also have influenced the siting of a nearby house (Fig 18), dated 1734, which was divided into two dwellings, perhaps for textile outworkers, at about the same time as the building of Garden Terrace. Syke Road still retains the character of a separate rural outworkers' hamlet, even though the subsequent growth of Manningham and Heaton has engulfed it.

The life of many textile outworkers in the late 18th and early 19th centuries was as different from that of their clothier predecessors as it was from that of contemporary and later factory workers. Although small by modern standards,

Figure 17
Garden Terrace, Heaton.
[DP071064]

Figure 18
A house of 1734 on Syke Road in Heaton which
has been converted into two dwellings.
[DP071542]

their houses were rarely shoddily built on the cheap and crowded into dirty town centres, but solid and often set within small shared garden grounds and surrounded by countryside. Life for the textile outworkers could be miserable at times and working hours were long but they were flexible and not governed by the rigid shift patterns of the mills. There was also no long trudge to work because the working and domestic environments were side by side. Now scattered, as though haphazardly, within a landscape of later, larger buildings and more regimented street planning, these plain outworkers' cottages and their shared gardens and yards recall a way of life in the textile districts of the West Riding which was once widespread. It was a life that could be remunerative at times but which, unable to compete with the increasing efficiency of the factory system, suffered a slow, painful extinction in the middle decades of the 19th century.

3

Manningham's Victorian heyday

The transformation of an outlying rural township close to a small Pennine market town into a densely built-up quarter of an industrial city is expressed starkly in maps – the wide open spaces of the largely agricultural landscape which had lingered until the 1840s were covered in housing, industrial buildings and suburban infrastructure by 1900 (Fig 19). It was a complex process however, and not simply the story of Bradford's outward expansion. Rather the change was brought about by a number of different forces and was manifested at different times in different ways. Dense industrial corridors developed on the south and east of the township, in the valleys of the Bradford Beck, while high-class residential areas were built closer to the old village at the township's heart. The different parts were ultimately linked by infill of different types. In places industry expanded to plant itself firmly in the heart of the township, and housing for many levels of society was built in an erratic pattern that at last eventually covered the vestiges of the township fields. Manningham ceased to be a semi-independent outlying township and became very much a part of Bradford – but one with a new and distinctive identity of its own.

However, Manningham in the 19th century was not a single suburb planned as a whole with consistent character, and for the most part the landscapes and buildings are not the product of an overall plan or a consistent direction of development. Instead it developed as a patchwork of areas whose distinctiveness is determined by the date of development, by intended function and social composition. Some important drivers of development are, however, evident, and this chapter will explore these. It will also consider the extent to which the different worlds of Victorian Manningham interacted. It was the successful men of commerce and trade who were instrumental in creating Manningham's dominant identity as the home of the wealthy, but the landscape was crowned by the iconic and awe-inspiring mass of Manningham Mills, and girdled by industrial development and workers' housing lower down on its west, south and east sides. Did lives lived in one environment significantly overlap with those lived in another, perhaps no more than a stone's throw away, or did they remain apart, orbiting a common centre but rarely, if ever, meeting? An examination of the complex process of suburb building, and of the lives of those who made the suburb their home, will help to answer these questions.

Figure 19
Detail from B Walker's 1882 Plan of the Borough of Bradford.
[Reproduced by permission of Bradford Libraries, Archives and Information Service, DP098011]

Villas and mills

In about 1832 – the year the great Reform Act made Bradford a parliamentary borough of which Manningham was part – John Garnett Horsfall (1788–1848), a worsted manufacturer with a mill in Bradford, built a villa for himself called Bolton Royd on the east side of Manningham Lane, at the top of the valley side and next to a little dell. The Horsfall family originally came from the nearby village of Denholme, where they made their money from coal, but John's father had been a cotton manufacturer and John had come to Bradford specifically to enter the worsted business, starting John Garnett Horsfall & Co in 1823. In 1825 he was the first to introduce steam-powered looms to the town, at his mill at North Wing, threatening the livelihoods of local handloom weavers.[5] The innovation precipitated several riots and attacks on the mill the following year resulting in several deaths. The smoke and noise of Bradford, not to mention the threat of violence in the town, no doubt led to Horsfall's decision to build a new home in the country. In 1830 the site for Horsfall's house was purchased from William Cowgill, a member of an old-established landowning Manningham family. When built, the Greek Revival-style house (Fig 20) was set within 35 acres (14.16ha) of grounds which sloped down the valley side to the Beck and Canal and was quite isolated from Bradford. The view to the east across the valley would have been stunning, as would the view north towards the River Aire. Moreover, there were no large textile mills in Manningham at that time (although a mill of some kind may have been operating at Brick Lane in the 1790s) – but this state of affairs would be fairly short-lived.

One of Horsfall's nearest neighbours was Ellis Cunliffe Lister (1774–1853) at Manningham Hall. Ellis Cunliffe of the Cunliffe family of Addingham had married into the Lister family, assumed their name, and inherited the Manningham estates from his wife in 1809. From 1815 to 1818 he built three textile mills, in Shipley, Great Horton and Bowling. While these were some distance from Manningham Hall, he evidently felt differently from Horsfall about the prospect of siting steam-powered factories close to his house because in 1838 (when following the Reform Act, he was one of Bradford's two new Members of Parliament) Lister built the first Manningham Mills out of stone from his own quarries at Daisy Hill. Originally called Lily Croft Mill, Lister's intention was that it should be run by his sons John and Samuel, and the latter

Figure 20
Bolton Royd, probably the first of a wave of rural villa residences to be built in Manningham for Bradford's new rich, was built in the early 1830s for a worsted manufacturer.
[DP071629]

oversaw construction of the mill which was built barely half a kilometre from Manningham Hall and equidistant from Manningham village. It occupied the same hilltop position as the present Manningham Mills and must have been clearly visible from the grounds of Lister's house, to which it was directly linked by Broad Lane (later renamed Victor Road). Samuel Cunliffe Lister also had two rows of workers' accommodation, of about 12 houses each, built close to the mill on its east side with one row immediately adjacent to the mill and the other fronting Heaton Road. Not only, therefore, was the large factory with its belching chimney virtually on the doorstep of Manningham Hall and its parkland but so were the homes of the workers employed there. If Horsfall had set a trend for the middle-class colonisation of Manningham's pastures for residential purposes (Manningham is still the most thinly populated of the four core townships, having, in 1834, only 3,564 inhabitants compared to Bowling's 5,958, Horton's 10,782 and Bradford's 23,223), then within a decade Lister had seemingly sown the seed of an industrial suburb consisting of factories and mass housing for the working class.

For the new rich who made their money in industrial Bradford the attraction of Manningham's elevated green fields was primarily as a quiet retreat from the dirt, smoke and squalor of the town. At the same time, Bradford itself was creeping northward towards the boundary with Manningham. Even as the merchants and manufacturers sought a rural idyll detached from the town, the 'best end' of Bradford was invading Manningham from the south where former fields were soon covered with terraces and, to a lesser extent, squares. Later decades saw new villas spring up, albeit to a denser pattern and within tightly circumscribed zones. But villa building now proceeded alongside the construction of growing numbers of back-to-back houses and small terraced houses. Some of these were occupied by workers in the mills and other factories that increasingly populated the valley floors and here and there dotted the higher ground, but overall they housed a surprisingly broad social range. By the end of the 19th century these disparate environments had joined together and much of the eastern third of the old township had been turned into what at first glance appears to have been a single suburb. The transformation was comprehensive, prompting local historian William Cudworth to remark in 1896 that 'in no other portion of the Borough of Bradford has such a material change been wrought'.[6]

The pioneering new rich

The majority of those who followed Horsfall's example, building villas overlooking the valley on the east side of Manningham Lane towards its northern end, were not only manufacturers but members of the new class of wealthy merchants who, along with professionals such as solicitors and bankers, began to flock to Bradford in the middle of the 19th century. By the 1830s Bradford's dominance of the worsted trade and the commercial success of its Piece Hall were such that it began to draw merchants away from the halls

Figure 21
Bradford Synagogue (Reform), Bowland Street, built in 1880. Bradford has the third oldest Reform community in the United Kingdom. The Bradford synagogue was designed by Francis and Thomas Healey of Bradford and is in Arabic ablaq style.
[AA038923]

at Wakefield, Halifax and even Leeds. It was said at the time that it was only the material existence of their mills, which could be neither moved nor disposed of, which stopped the manufacturers from following suit.[7] There was a substantial influx of merchants from Leeds especially and among them were the first German Jewish merchants. They would have an important influence on Bradford's trade throughout the rest of the 19th century, conferring their identity on the district of fine warehouses and offices close to the centre of town that became known as 'Little Germany'. So significant was their presence in Manningham that in 1880 Bradford's first synagogue (Fig 21 and *see* Fig 99) was built here on Bowland Street. It was financed by Bernard Cohen, head of Charles Semon & Company, worsted merchants, who lived at Blenheim Mount on Manningham Lane.

Bradford's merchants, both British and foreign, became the town's aristocracy and played a major part in its governance. Few of them cared to dwell in the town centre, however, even if initially only the top echelon had the means to live elsewhere. During the 1840s and 1850s, a period during which Bradford, Manningham, Horton and Bowling combined (in 1847) to form a new municipal borough of Bradford, a number of large, elegantly classical villas were built in the vicinity of Bolton Royd. A new and tranquil suburb of superior residences, each set in fine grounds on the edge of a green valley, was established on the east side of Manningham Lane (Fig 22). Here, as elsewhere in the township, agricultural land was divided into narrow, individually owned strip-shaped fields, stretching from the Lane all the way down to the Beck, making neat land parcels which were eminently suitable for villa building and the laying out of streets. Horsfall's Bolton Royd was followed by Rose Mount Villa (Fig 23), situated a little to the south and built in 1849 for John Douglas, a wealthy Bradford merchant, while still further south Jacob Philipp, a German-born merchant, built the stately Clifton House in 1851 (Fig 24). Both houses were designed by Andrews and Delauney, one of Bradford's many emerging and increasingly celebrated architectural practices, whose enduring works would lend Manningham, and Bradford, much of its strong home-grown character.

As more of Bradford's successful merchants sought to live in the area, its character began to change and the spacious grounds of some early villas were parcelled up as new building land. For example, in about the early 1850s Parkfield House (Fig 25) was built, on a portion of the Bolton Royd estate that

Figure 22
The Ordnance Survey map of 1893 showing the villa suburb on the east side of Manningham Lane.

Figure 23
Rose Mount Villa was built in 1849 for a successful Bradford merchant named John Douglas.
[DP071617]

Figure 24
Clifton House, Clifton Villas.
[DP071537]

Figure 25
With a large circular carriage drive at its front, the setting of the classically styled and proportioned Parkfield House exemplifies the villa dwellers' desire for seclusion.
[DP071832]

Figure 26
No. 8 Clifton Villas which has been Bradford's Estonian
social and cultural club, Eesti Kodu,
for over half a century.
[DP071567]

Figure 27
A plan of No. 8 Clifton Villas and grounds, built in
the 1850s. Three sizeable reception rooms were
supplemented by an extensive set of bedrooms and
service rooms including staff bedrooms in the attics.
There was a formal front garden and a stable, trap
house and greenhouses in the grounds.

had been sold off after Horsfall's death in 1848. Its owner was Sir Henry
Mitchell, then a leading merchant with the worsted firm of A & S Henry &
Co (whose Bradford branch was on Leeds Road, on the edge of Little
Germany), and later one of Bradford's leading inhabitants, becoming mayor
and a Justice of the Peace. His new house stood less than 100m from Bolton
Royd, though its arrangement, facing northwards across a formal front
garden with circular carriage drive, still reflected the villa-owner's
customary desire for seclusion. Clifton House, in contrast, was part of a
gated enclave of – at its fullest extent – about 10 similar houses lining a
private street called Clifton Villas (Fig 26). Few of these were as large as
Clifton House, and most of them were in surprisingly close proximity to each
other in diminutive but, in time, well-wooded grounds. No. 8 Clifton Villas
(Fig 27), to take one example, is set slightly further back than most of the
others and, like Parkfield House, had a formal front garden but only a small
rear service yard containing a detached stable and trap house (Fig 28).
Remarkably for such a well-appointed residence, the yard and stable backed
directly onto a deep but disused stone quarry – a legacy of one of
Manningham's earlier industries. Bolton Royd and Parkfield House were
themselves engulfed a decade after the building of Clifton Villas when the

Figure 28
The trap house and stable to the rear of No. 8 Clifton
Villas.
[DP071571]

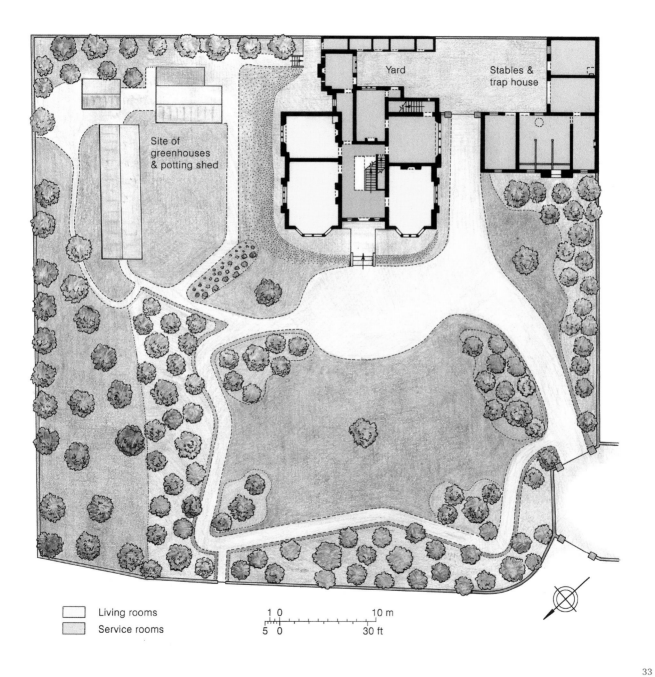

Yard

Stables & trap house

Site of
greenhouses
& potting shed

Living rooms

Service rooms

1 0   10 m

5 0   30 ft

Figure 29
Oak Well is one of the more architecturally distinctive villas on Oak Avenue. It was built in 1864 but enlarged in 1888. [DP071831]

Figure 30
This six-pointed star is part of the barge-boarding on the gable at the front of Oak Hurst, Oak Avenue, perhaps commemorating the German-Jewish origin of the original owner.
[DP071793]

Figure 31
Part of the second-floor interior of No. 8 Clifton Villas showing the servants' landing.
[DP071560]

Oak House Estate, named after an earlier house close to Bolton Royd, was bought and laid out for development in 1864 by the Oak Mount Building Club and the Oak Villas Building Club. They built semi-detached villas on the two parallel streets between Oak Avenue and Parkfield Road that bear their names. Oak Avenue itself was left with large open plots on which wealthier individuals were free to build their own bespoke houses (Figs 29 and 30).

From its origins as an isolated rural villa set in its own extensive grounds, Bolton Royd had become, in just a generation, part of a much more tightly planned, though still select, suburban neighbourhood stretching along the east side of Manningham Lane all the way from Clifton Street to Cunliffe Road. Opulent detached and semi-detached villas were grouped in self-contained enclaves, often gated to ensure exclusivity. Despite the tendency for classical detailing and proportions to be superseded by brash, often Gothic, designs incorporating asymmetrical facades, high porches and turrets, steeply pitched gables and elaborate barge-boarding, these enclaves nevertheless formed a larger district of cohesive character. Life would have been peaceful and pleasant for the villa owners and their families in an exclusive garden suburb among neighbours who were social equals and most likely in the same line of business. It is worth remembering, however, that most such residences were occupied by substantial households by today's standards and were designed to include servants' accommodation and a range of service rooms. According to the census returns for 1881, for example, Jacob Philipp, who was by then a widower and was described as a 'Commission Merchant', lived at Clifton House with his son Charles, also a 'Commission Merchant', supported by a housekeeper, a cook, a housemaid and a general servant – all of them female. In the same year, Sarah Calvert, a widow, lived three doors down at No. 8 Clifton Villas without any family but with the assistance of two live-in female servants. These lists of servants serve to remind us that in the realm of the better-off, separate worlds existed even within single residences and it is wrong to think of the exclusive enclaves of the rich as theirs alone. In reality most were outnumbered in their own homes by those of lower class whom they employed – the butlers, housekeepers, cooks and housemaids who inhabited the same buildings and places but an entirely different world, unable to 'own' and enjoy their surroundings in the same way as their employers (Fig 31).

The succession of middle orders

Further south, the town was invading the Manningham countryside. By the mid-1830s the ribbon development along Westgate, which had begun before 1800, had joined White Abbey, through Black Abbey, to Bradford. Some of the houses were perhaps small rows of cottages built by mill owners for their workers but, by the 1840s, new building land was being sought for better-quality housing between Lumb Lane and Manningham Lane – and no wonder. The centre of Bradford by the mid-1840s had seemingly become intolerable for anyone who could afford to choose where they lived. Friedrich Engels described it as enveloped in a grey cloud of coal smoke on weekdays, with filth and debris lying in heaps in courts and alleys.[8] According to Engels, the houses were ruinous, dirty and miserable, the worst being the working men's cottages amongst the mills at the valley bottom. He described the Beck itself as a coal-black, foul-smelling stream. Although Engels' political agenda may have influenced his tone, there is little doubt that Bradford had deteriorated in the couple of decades since the observations in Baines's *Directory* of 1822 although there were some areas of good housing to the south. This view is reinforced by the observations of A B Reach, a correspondent for the London newspaper the *Morning Chronicle*, who was chosen to undertake an investigation into the condition of the working classes in the north of Britain as part of a nationwide survey. Reach described Bradford as, with a few exceptions, an 'accumulation of mean streets, steep lanes, and huge mills intersected here and there by … odious patches of black, muddy, vast ground rooted by pigs, and strewn with oyster-shells, cabbage-stalks, and such garbage …'.[9]

Only the wealthiest could afford to join the likes of Horsfall, Douglas and Philipp by buying land and building a villa on the green slopes near Bolton Royd. For those of lesser means a way out lay in clubbing together to form building societies, which could then buy land and construct houses commensurate with their members' wealth. Building societies were a more sophisticated version of the earlier building 'club' system. They had been operating for some years under the Friendly Societies Act of 1793, but increased greatly in number following the 1832 Reform Act and were officially recognised by the Regulation of Benefit Building Societies Act in 1836. Many of the societies operating in Bradford at this time were 'terminating', rather than 'permanent'

Figure 32
Nos. 229–33 Manningham Lane are amongst the earliest higher-status terraced houses in Manningham.
[DP071802]

(although the latter did begin to appear in the mid-1840s). Terminating societies provided their members with the money to build houses, winding up once every member's mortgage was paid and their debts discharged. The membership was drawn principally, but not exclusively, from Bradford's growing lower middle-class tier of managers and successful tradesmen; the terraces they built were sometimes around modest squares, firstly in the rural fringe still separating Bradford from Manningham township, and then within the township itself, largely in a corridor between Lumb Lane and Manningham Lane and on the east side of Manningham Lane at its southern end.

The development process, whether driven by building societies or private speculators, was steady but piecemeal with fields being typically sold off for development one by one rather than in large blocks. This resulted in new streets and squares appearing here and there, often separated from each other by remaining fields but always connecting with established main roads, which themselves became lined with terraces on plot edges. Although these developments mostly occurred between the 1840s and 1860s, the first terraces of this kind in Manningham were in fact built in the early 1830s on the west side of Manningham Lane – Nos. 229–33 (Fig 32), just south of the later

Walmer Villas, and at Spring Gardens. They were followed in the 1840s by those at Eldon Place and Hanover Square (Figs 33 and 34), both between Lumb Lane and Manningham Lane. Most of the larger developments were built by building societies – for example, in 1851 the Crown Building Society built Peel Square (Fig 35) and a decade later the Hallfield Building Society erected the terraced houses of Hallfield Road (Fig 36).

These ventures constituted a new suburb on what were now the outskirts of Bradford, and separate from the growing villa settlement to the north with which it made a striking contrast. This was not a world of villas, leafy gardens and fine views, but of terraced houses grouped around 'squares' of varying regularity, open streets and even crescents and all speaking the formal and repetitive architectural language of the town. In contrast to the villa settlement it was within easy walking distance of the business district, and few of the houses were equipped with private stables and coach or trap houses. It was distant enough however to merit its own church (something Manningham village would not receive for another five years): St Jude's was built in 1843, just to the north of Hanover Square and just within Manningham township.

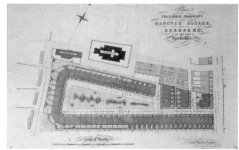

Figure 33
The horseshoe-shaped Hanover Square was built in Bradford, immediately south of the border with Manningham township.
[NMR/20851/023]

Figure 34
Plan of freeholds at Hanover Square, Joseph Smith, Land Agent and Surveyor. It is dated April 1852 and also shows the outline of St Jude's Church and Schools.
[Reproduced by permission of Bradford Libraries, Archives and Information Service, DP098001]

Figure 35 (top)
Peel Square is not a square but only half of one.
It was the work of the Crown Building Society
and is dated 1851.
[DP071657]

Figure 36 (above)
Hallfield Road originally linked Lumb Lane with Manningham Lane and the houses
which terminate the terraces at the west end are designed to resemble detached
villas and face Lumb Lane. The eastern half of the road was once lined with the
Bradford Eye & Ear Hospital, a large Baptist chapel and the girls' grammar school.
Hallfield Road now terminates at Houghton Place and the hospital, chapel and school
have all been demolished. [DP071647]

Schools were added in 1846 – important steps towards attaining that degree of self-sufficiency which is the mark of the mature suburb.

Other pockets of building society development, isolated from the immediate vicinity of Hanover Square, followed to the north and closer to Manningham village. Southfield Square (Fig 37), for example, was built in 1853–65 by the Southfield Place and Laburnum Building Society on the west side of Lumb Lane, where it occupied part of the old 'South Field', one of the Manningham's ancient town fields. Even though it is the most conventional in appearance of Manningham's 'squares', the attractive two-storeyed terraced houses only line three sides of a large elongated rectangle containing allotment gardens. To its east was Apsley Crescent (Fig 38), built in 1852 to designs by Andrews and Delauney by the Apsley Land Society which also built the

Figure 37
Southfield Square takes it name from the 'South Field', one of Manningham township's historic town fields on which it was partly built.
[DP071658]

Figure 38
Apsley Crescent, built by the Apsley Land Society.
[DP071806]

adjoining Mornington and Walmer Villas (Fig 39) – all part of a series of developments which included Wellesley Terrace, Mornington Place, Walmer Place, Marlborough Place and a number of houses fronting Marlborough Road and Blenheim Road. The shallow Apsley Crescent and the partially demolished Wellesley Terrace take their concentric shape from a bow in the line of Lumb Lane. Terraces not built around squares were lent exclusivity by being set back from the road and by the provision of shared but private gated carriage drives such as at Blenheim Mount (Fig 40), a fine and substantial terrace of 11 three-storeyed houses built in 1865 beside the increasingly busy Manningham Lane. Unified in name by homage to the Dukes of Wellington and Marlborough, this was a denser development than that on the east side of Manningham Lane –

Figure 39
Plan of sites for residences at Apsley Crescent, Walmer Villas and Mornington Villas by Joseph Smith dated 3 August 1853.
[Reproduced by permission of Bradford Libraries, Archives and Information Service, DP098012]

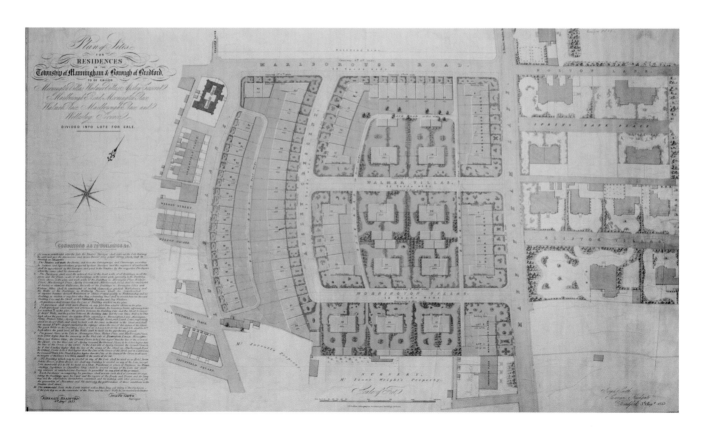

Figure 40
Blenheim Mount. Built in about 1865, Blenheim Mount is set back from the bustling Manningham Lane and was served by a private carriage drive. [DP071550]

Figure 41
Fairmount, beside North Park Road (originally called Hesp Lane). Fairmount faced directly towards Manningham Hall across the Low Park and was one of the first residential developments to take advantage of this seemingly protected view.
[DP071582]

even in its later phases – but one whose layout nevertheless shielded it from neighbouring areas of lesser housing.

The Lumb Lane–Manningham Lane corridor reached as far as the western fringes of the grounds of Manningham Hall, which offered potential residents an attractive and seemingly protected prospect. One of the first additions to this area was Fairmount (Fig 41) – a terrace of six houses built as a speculation in 1853 by J W Mills, a merchant turned property developer who lived at Hanover Square. When built, Fairmount stood in virtual isolation and faced slightly west of north, directly towards Manningham Hall (Fig 42). By the end of the 19th century the surrounding streets and houses stretched up the hill as far as Manningham Mills. The catalyst for much of this development came in 1870 when Lister moved to Farfield Hall near Addingham and sold Manningham Hall, together with the former Low and Deer Parks, to the Corporation of Bradford at a discount price on condition that the land was used as a public park. By this seemingly altruistic act Lister provided Manningham with a second great landmark in the form of Lister Park. He had in fact earlier intended to develop the land for housing, as is clearly indicated by a plan of 1869 by Gay and Swallow, architects and surveyors of Bradford, showing 100 'villa' residences – detached, semi-detached and in terraces of three and four – in a dispersed

Figure 42
Detail from Thomas Dixon's 1844–6 map of Bradford (revised and corrected to 1856) showing Fairmount before the development of the surrounding area. The small quarries depicted to the front and rear of the row may have been the source of the building stone. [Reproduced by permission of Bradford Libraries, Archives and Information Service, DP098007]

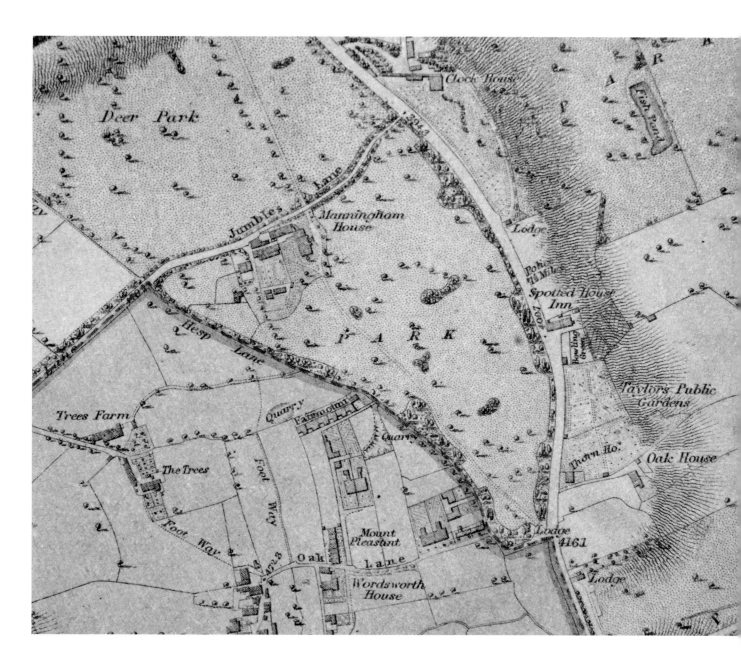

Figure 43
Gay and Swallow's 1869 plan of Manningham Park
showing a scheme for villa residences. It is not widely
known that early plans for the Manningham Park estate
involved the construction of 100 such houses, covering the
entire park, rather than its sale to Bradford as a public
amenity.
[Reproduced by permission of Bradford Libraries,
Archives and Information Service, DP098002]

pattern linked by looping drives (Fig 43). It is not clear why Lister ultimately decided against the scheme. It might have been that the demand for such villa residences was falling away by this time, although they continued to be built in smaller numbers elsewhere in the area, while demand for smaller houses increased as the lower classes took their turn to colonise Manningham.

Housing Manningham's lower classes

A large number of the smaller houses with which Manningham filled up in the middle and later decades of the 19th century were terraced and back-to-backs – a type once common in some northern English towns and cities because they were cheaper to build than 'through-houses' and provided more rental income from a smaller area of land. Rows of single-celled back-to-back houses were built in Bradford up until 1860 (in 1854 three-quarters of the new houses for which approval was granted were of back-to-back type) but very few dwellings of this vintage survive. By the middle of the 19th century, however, back-to-back houses had become associated with insanitary conditions and widespread ill health and were falling into disrepute. The building of new back-to-back houses was banned in Bradford in 1860, but the move was so unpopular that the ban was relaxed just five years later, though subject to tight new building by-laws. These specified that the new houses had to have sufficient space to their fronts and sides, or be built in units of four with a central ground-floor through-passage or 'tunnel' that had to be at least 6ft 6ins (1.98m) wide and 8ft (2.4m) high in order to allow an ash cart to back through it. The two front houses faced the street, sometimes overlooking small forecourts, while the rear houses opened on to a communal yard or garden at the bottom of which were privy blocks shared by all four houses.

Manningham's suburban development prior to 1860 had been largely driven by the needs of the wealthier middle classes, and hardly any back-to-back houses without tunnels, of the type popularly associated with urban slum conditions, were built in Manningham. Of the back-to-back houses built near Manningham village, on what became Ambler Street and on Bavaria Place, all have been demolished except for four at the north-west end of Bavaria Place, which bear a name plate and the date 1847 (Figs 44 and 45). The tunnel back-to-backs built in Manningham – and there were hundreds of them by the end of the century, next to the mansions and villas of the very best areas, close to Manningham Mills, to the west of Manningham village, in Lumb Lane and in Girlington – were relatively spacious and comfortable. The best often had

Figure 44 (above)
Most of the earlier type of back-to-back houses, those without tunnels, which were built before 1860 have been swept away. This 1847 remnant on Bavaria Place is therefore a rare survivor.
[DP065774]

Figure 45 (right)
All that remains of the back-to-back houses which once lined Bavaria Place, Silver Street and Anvil Street.
[DP065775]

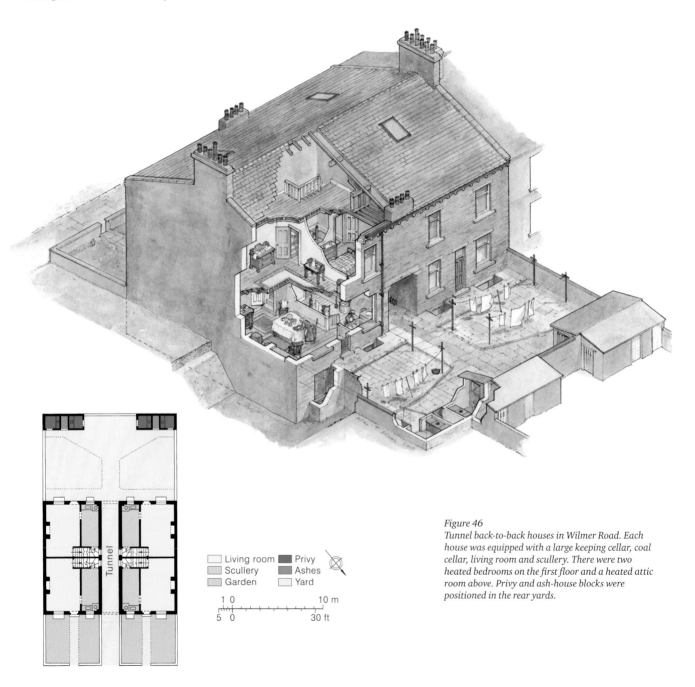

Living room   Privy
Scullery   Ashes
Garden   Yard

1 0   10 m
5 0   30 ft

Figure 46
Tunnel back-to-back houses in Wilmer Road. Each house was equipped with a large keeping cellar, coal cellar, living room and scullery. There were two heated bedrooms on the first floor and a heated attic room above. Privy and ash-house blocks were positioned in the rear yards.

accommodation on three floors, so there was ample room for children, plus a keeping cellar, pantry, coal store (filled through a ground-level hatch in the tunnel wall) and a scullery (Fig 46). A lesser version was only equipped with a sink at the top of the cellar stairs, known as the 'cellar head', instead of a scullery. Many different types of people, from the families of mill workers to successful artisans, tradesmen and even schoolteachers, lived in these houses which were a far cry from the unregulated back-to-back slums that were the blight of some industrial cities at the time. Few such households, if any, could afford servants, however, and it was not uncommon for incomes to be supplemented by a lodger. For example, the census returns for 1891 tell us that the household at No. 29 Wilmer Road (one of a row of better back-to-back houses built in the 1880s) was headed by Frankland Greenwood, a plush finisher (presumably at Manningham Mills), who lived with his wife Mary without children but with a lodger named Joshua Jenkinson who was aged just 16 at the time and worked as a gardener. The neighbours at No. 25 were Albert Rushton, a mechanic (fitter), who lived with his wife Esther, son Harry and daughter Beatrice, while at No. 31 Martha Ideson, a widow of 73, lived with her daughters Hannah and Emma (a velvet weaver), and 18-year-old grandson Arthur Bradham (a clerk).

The concentration of back-to-back houses in Girlington, west of Manningham village, is the outcome of a particularly interesting social and political experiment by the Bradford Equitable Building Society and Freehold Land Society, established in 1849. Freehold land societies were formed to help working men own their own houses by freehold – and so qualify for the vote – thanks to the retention, in the 1832 Reform Act, of the right of any county freeholder with property worth more than 40 shillings (£2) to vote in county elections, including those who lived in a parliamentary borough within the county. The first such society was formed in Birmingham in 1847 and many more sprang up throughout the provinces in the following few years. The Bradford society was presided over by Titus Salt and its committee members included a number of leading local industrialists such as Joseph Nutter and Joseph Illingworth. Salt was an extremely successful Bradford cloth manufacturer, specialising in alpaca production, and an energetic philanthropist. In 1848–9 he served as Bradford's mayor and starting in the early 1850s he famously built a large new mill and model village for his

Figure 47
Bradford Tradesmen's Homes at Lily Croft. The Bradford Tradesmen's Homes were built in two phases in the 1860s and 1870s for old tradesmen, pensioners of the Tradesmen's Benevolent Society, who, through no fault of their own, had fallen on hard times. They are an attractive group of four rows of almshouses with an integral chapel.
[DP065421]

Figure 48
The interior of the chapel in the centre of the main range at the Bradford Tradesmen's Homes, Lily Croft.
[DP065422]

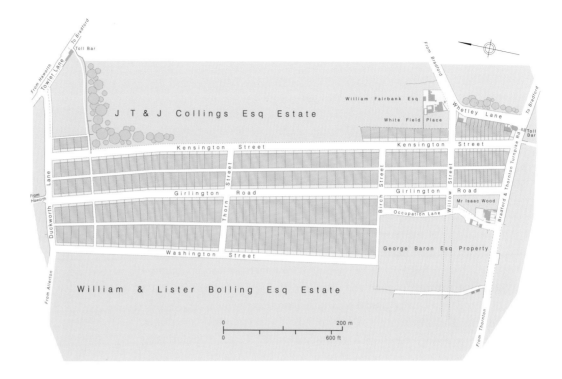

Figure 49
Plan of the Bradford Freehold Land Society's Girlington estate as laid out for sale, based on a sales plan of January 1852 by surveyor Joseph Smith.

workers at Saltaire near Shipley, outside Bradford borough whose problems of pollution and overcrowding Salt did not wish to exacerbate. Salt was also the driving force and chief benefactor of the later Bradford Tradesmen's Homes at Lily Croft (Figs 47 and 48).

The purpose of the Bradford Freehold Land Society was to form a single common fund from the contributions of its members, and use it to purchase large areas of land suitable for building which would then be parcelled up, either to be let on building leases or else developed by individual society members. By this method the society estimated that it could reduce the cost of acquiring a qualifying freehold franchise from £70 to just £20. The society purchased a narrow and roughly rectangular tract between Duckworth Lane and Thornton Road, Girlington, during 1850–2, and proceeded to lay out long streets aligned north to south following the steep gradient of the valley side (Fig 49). This was a truly pioneering suburb in that it was set well apart from the existing built-up area. Development of the estate was slow, however, partly because of poor drainage on the site and partly due to lack of demand. In spite of its proximity to the factories which would later line Thornton Road, Girlington attracted not the working-class men that it was intended for but rather the lower-middle classes, artisans, shopkeepers and so on. Even the right of residents to the franchise was quashed when a ruling of 1855 declared that building society mortgage holders did not qualify. For decades Girlington remained separated from Manningham and Bradford by fields, and despite the building of a church (St Philip's, 1859–60) it must have seemed an isolated and ill-equipped community for some years with limited social provision at first. It did receive more social provision in time however. The Ordnance Survey map of 1893 shows two public houses, Methodist and Baptist chapels (both with Sunday schools), a branch of the Bradford Free Library and Board schools for boys, girls and infants. Tram services would arrive later.

A significant number of tunnel back-to-back houses in Manningham were built by the Bradford Provident and Industrial Society Limited (BPISL) which was Bradford's main co-operative society (it later became the City of Bradford Co-operative Society Limited). As well as building and running co-operative stores, such as Branch No. 37 on Manningham Lane (Fig 50), it built houses and offered them for sale or rent on reasonable terms, in contrast to the high prices charged by private landlords. The BPISL was formed following the 1862 Industrial and Provident Societies Act which empowered a society registered under it to 'purchase, erect, and sell, and convey, or to hold lands and buildings'. The BPISL built a substantial number of tunnel back-to-backs in Manningham in the 1880s and 1890s, often in terraces that included a large co-operative store, such as the block of four houses built beside a large shop and warehouse on Firth Road in Heaton (Fig 51). Most of the houses on Leamington Street, Victor Street and Victor Terrace, immediately east of Manningham Mills, were built by the BIPSL. In 1898 the houses of Victor Terrace were inhabited by households headed by clerks, commercial travellers and tradesmen and also included a manager, a toy merchant and one individual styling himself 'gentleman'.

As with so many of Manningham's inhabitants, the lives of those who lived in its back-to-back and modest through-houses would have been quite insular. Social circles probably revolved around church or chapel while family members living nearby would have been all-important in the day-to-day lives of wives and children: few, if any, households would have included servants. The occupational range of the heads of households would have been relatively wide however. The families of lesser employees in the textile trades were the neighbours of schoolteachers, textile-mill overlookers (shop-floor supervisors),

Figure 50
The Bradford Provident and Industrial Society's Branch
No. 37 on Manningham Lane.
[DP071060]

Figure 51
The Bradford Provident and Industrial Society's store and group of four back-to-back houses on the corner of Heaton Road and Firth Road in Heaton.
[DP065783]

commercial travellers, shopkeepers, mechanics, pattern designers, wheelwrights, stone masons and dressmakers (to choose but a few of the inhabitants of Wilmer Road in 1891) and, because of the isolating effect of their length, streets very often defined secular micro-communities, creating more worlds within worlds.

Industrial development

When he built Lily Croft Mill, Ellis Cunliffe Lister might have sown the seeds of a new industrial suburb of Bradford, but instead Manningham developed substantially as a collection of mostly middle-class residential suburbs and industry was largely confined to the periphery in two industrial corridors which bordered the residential districts. Nevertheless, the mills were a substantial presence in the later 19th-century township – sometimes encroaching on the homes of the well-to-do and sometimes strongly influencing new middle-class housing – and contributed much to its overall character, life and prosperity. For Bradford's merchants Manningham was a place they could retire to at the end of the working day to escape the smoke of factories and bustle of town, but many established residents, like the Listers, saw business opportunities in the emerging suburb itself. It is not surprising – the mid-19th century was a time of rapid economic advancement in Bradford and there was a period of expansion from roughly 1850–70 during which many fortunes were made. Powered weaving had been perfected earlier in the century, following the pioneering work of Edmund Cartwright in the 1780s. One component of the worsted industry – wool combing – was not successfully mechanised until the 1840s, however, when Ellis Cunliffe Lister's son Samuel developed an efficient machine for the job, providing a great boost to Bradford's worsted industry. Such the profits to be made that Lister converted his Manningham Mill entirely to wool combing and let space there to tenants at high prices. Trade was further boosted by the opening of the Leeds and Bradford Railway in 1846 which meant that Bradford goods could be sent more quickly to Leeds for export to the Continent. The new railway line followed the Bradford Canal and Beck north to Shipley before turning east for Leeds along the Aire Valley, thus avoiding the steep hills that otherwise ringed Bradford. Further advances, including the opening of the Bradford Wool Exchange in 1867, encouraged further industrial expansion and during the second half of the 19th century more factories, worsted mills, cotton mills and wool-combing works were built in Manningham, encroaching closely on the establishing residential districts and of course seeding new industrial suburban zones with houses for the working population.

By the 1840s, Brick Lane Mill and Low Globe Mill, both worsted manufactories, were operating in Manningham between City Road and White Abbey Road. Later they were joined in the White Abbey and Thornton Road area (once called Lower Globe) by Whetley Mills in 1863–5 (Fig 52), Oakwood Dye Works and a rebuilt Brick Lane Mills (Fig 53). To the south of Thornton Road, in the bottom of the valley, Brown Royd developed as a small industrial suburb in its own right with, by the end of the century, numerous factories and six streets of tunnel back-to-back housing. Adjacent to the east was Alston

Figure 52
Whetley Mills were a steam-powered worsted-spinning works built in 1863. Unusually the complex was equipped with its own wool-combing shed.
[DP071668]

Figure 53
The present Brick Lane Mills were built in the mid-19th century and consisted of two spinning blocks, weaving sheds, two engine houses, three warehouses, offices and of course a chimney. Unfortunately they have been reduced to a burnt-out shell.
[DP071983]

Works while further west Cumberland Works, another large wool-combing works, was established in 1875 close to Four Lane Ends. Altogether these formed a great chimney-masted slab across the southern edge of Manningham, very different from the suburbs to the north and east into which they intruded. James Drummond's Lumb Lane Mills (Fig 54) is particularly incongruous. It stands slightly apart from the great valley-bottom concentration of factories, almost immediately opposite the rear of Hanover Square, and the mill's tall chimney dominates the view into Hanover Square from Manningham Lane (Fig 55). The mills were constructed from 1856–69, barely a decade after Hanover Square, and where once would have been green fields was now the smoke and noise of a steam-powered factory, and the regular tramp of workers in and out along Lumb Lane.

The first mill on Manningham's eastern side was erected in 1851, again in the valley bottom. Valley Mills (Fig 56), on the Manningham side of the township boundary, was a steam-powered cotton and worsted mill and was owned, but only partly occupied, by Samuel Sutcliffe and Sons, cotton spinners. Three streets of back-to-back houses, predating the by-law of 1860 and so without tunnels, were built for the workers south-east of the mills in Valley Row, Valley Street and Hopwood Street. Valley Mills were soon joined by Ingham's Dye Works. By the end of the century the view into the valley, which once attracted residents to the hillside above, consisted of an industrial corridor stretching all the way into Bradford and including a cotton factory, wool-combing sheds, a gas works, and from 1872, Manningham Motive Power Depot, a huge complex of sidings, engine sheds and even livestock pens and a slaughter house. Much of the residential development of the suburb occurred simultaneously with the emergence of this industrial corridor; the fact that the railway interposed an impermeable barrier between them doubtless helped to sustain the genteel life of Manningham's villas in the sight of the contrasting world of factories and workers' houses beyond.

Manningham Mills

Lister's Manningham Mills and their part in the story of Manningham differ substantially from that of the industrial corridors to the south and east. In 1871, the old Manningham Mill at Lily Croft, which by then had been turned to silk production, burned to the ground, taking with it much of Samuel Lister's

Figure 54
James Drummond's Lumb Lane Mills, built between 1856 and 1869.
[DP071654]

Figure 55
The chimney of Lumb Lane Mills is clearly visible from Hanover Square.
[DP071593]

Figure 56
Valley Mills was the first industrial complex to be built in Manningham beside the eastern arm of the Bradford Beck, in the middle of the 19th century. It is also the only survivor.
[DP071661]

Figure 57
An aerial view of Samuel Cunliffe Lister's Manningham
Mills taken in 1974 when the complex was still more or
less in full production. Two years later Manningham Mills
proudly produced new velvet curtains to hang in the
historic Treaty Room of the White House.
[NMR/af103/aerofilms/ac274071]

Figure 58
An aerial view of Manningham Mills taken in 2008
showing restoration and conversion work by Urban
Splash in progress.
[NMR/20851/055]

pioneering textile machinery, including his silk-combing machine and an experimental power loom for silk which was nearing perfection. Undismayed, and undeterred by the slump in trade which followed the ending of the Franco-Prussian War, Lister began almost immediately to build the present Manningham Mills, which mostly date from 1872 to 1888, on the site of the old factory. When complete the new Manningham Mills (Fig 57) was the largest silk-spinning and weaving mill in Great Britain, employing as many as 11,000 at its height. Its visual impact is hard to over-emphasise. With its colossal chimney, it was and is a prominent and architecturally lavish eye-catcher, seemingly intended by Lister to be as much a visual asset to the residential neighbourhood as the park which bore his name. From a distance it appears monstrous yet coherent, while at close quarters it seems endless but impressive with startling variations in scale and repetitive but well-proportioned detailing to the various elevations. It is another part of Manningham in its own right and one which, like all the others with which it so superbly blends, was built to last (Fig 58).

During the following three decades the space between Lister Park and the new Manningham Mills was subject to rapid development, filling with new housing ranging from detached villas to tunnel back-to-backs, as well as shops (on Oak Lane) and places of worship. Little of the housing was for those who worked at the Mills, for whom tunnel back-to-back houses were built on the Mills' west side where Patent and Silk Streets, for example, bear testimony to the employer of the inhabitants. In contrast, the strip to the immediate south-west of Lister Park was populated by large semi-detached villas and terraces of mansions, most of which faced the Park across North Park Road. Around Heaton Reservoir (completed in 1857 and an attractive feature in its own right) and the parkland surrounding Heaton Hall, villa development extended as far as Emm Lane.

In marked contrast as the land rose south-westwards towards the Mills the quality of the houses declined in proportion to their distance from Lister Park. Here the transitions that recur so often in Manningham are compressed into the space of a few hundred metres. Parts of streets close to the Park were lined with long terraces of substantial houses, distinguished by decorative barge-boarding, and there was also a small development of semi-detached villas, centred on Ashburnham Grove but also lining part of Park View Road and the north-east side of Birr Road. Houses such as these would have been the homes of families

Figure 59
No. 12 Park View Road is a large semi-detached villa and one of a number built in a small cluster close to Lister Park. This view is from Birr Road.
[DP071692]

Figure 60
*One of the fine ground-floor rooms at
No. 12 Park View Road.
[DP071701]*

Figure 61
*The first-floor landing at No. 12 Park View Road,
with bedrooms to the left and a staircase to the
right leading to second-floor bedrooms for
children and servants.
[DP071703]*

of textile merchants, wealthy professionals and gentlemen and ladies of independent means, but their households typically included fewer live-in servants than those of the earlier detached villas on the east side of Manningham Lane. According to the census returns of 1901, No. 12 Park View Road (Figs 59–61), for example, was the home of Hugo Eylert, a German yarn merchant who lived there with his wife and two daughters with the help of just a cook and a housemaid. With spacious ground- and first-floor family rooms, a large kitchen, service basement and second-floor servants' accommodation, the

Figure 62
Lilycroft Board School faces Manningham Mills across Lilycroft Road and is an early Bradford Board school built in 1872–3.
[DP071984]

Figure 63
The Belle Vue Higher Grade Schools were built in 1895 by the Bradford School Board.
[DP071717]

Figure 64
The Belle Vue public house on Manningham Lane, which was at times notorious for public drunkenness.
[DP071723]

house was clearly designed with the well-off in mind – yet Manningham Mills is close by. They loom large behind St John's Chapel in the view from the front garden of the house and dominate that from the upper-floor windows, although the bulk of the Mills is balanced by the view of Bolton Heights to the east. Further from the Park lesser houses were built higher up on Victor Road and the side streets to the south are lined with back-to-back housing. But even if some regarded the presence of the Mills as an unwelcome reminder of the necessity of labour, its potential as a visual embellishment was evidently recognised by the developers because both Victor Road and Selborne Terrace are aligned with its gargantuan Italianate chimney, making it clearly visible from Lister Park.

Life in Victorian Manningham

Much of Manningham's late 19th-century landscape still survives and we can see the streets and buildings where the people of Manningham lived, were educated, worked and spent their leisure time – the houses, schools, factories, parks, pubs and so on. Far harder to perceive are the more intimate details of their day-to-day lives and it can be difficult to imagine to what extent, and in what circumstances, their lives intersected or diverged. Manningham was not simply a dormitory for Bradford's commercial centre, a place for businessmen to commute from, although that was certainly one of its major roles, but a place separate from Bradford and to some degree self-contained. Manningham was watched over by its own police station (*see* Fig 93) and had its own schools, most of them built by the Bradford School Board, such as Lily Croft Board School (Fig 62) on Lilycroft Road which was built in the early 1870s and the large higher grade schools (Fig 63) of 1895 on the corner of Belle Vue and Manningham Lane. Schools, especially the non-denominational Board schools, exercised a powerful unifying influence on communities. So too, though less demonstratively, did the shopping centres on Oak Lane and Carlisle Road, which catered for essentially local needs, and the wider range of shops on Manningham Lane, which appealed not only to locals but to residents of other parts of Bradford and to the traffic passing along such a major thoroughfare. The places of entertainment, such as the now-demolished Theatre Royal and the Belle Vue public house (Fig 64), both on Manningham

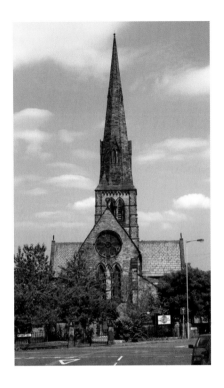

Lane, were also vibrant meeting places for certain sectors of Manningham society. Manningham also possessed facilities which drew in a wider public, like Lister Park, and some which met the needs of Bradford as a whole and even beyond. It was home to the Bradford Children's Hospital (*see* Fig 92) and St Catherine's Home for Incurables (1898), among many health and welfare institutions, to the city's grammar school and, from 1904, its art gallery and museum. It also became the home of Bradford City Football Club in 1903.

Given the sectarian nature of Victorian religious life, Manningham's numerous places of worship could unite communities only within the confines of a single faith or sect, though they had the power to transcend social barriers in a way that many 19th-century institutions could not. But there was no church in Manningham until St Jude's was completed in 1843 next to Hanover Square, at a cost of £3,000. It was followed in 1847 by St Paul's, Manningham's new parish church at the heart of the old village (Fig 65), which was built thanks to the single benefaction of one man, John Hollings. As the century progressed more and more places of worship were built, underlining the importance of religious life and telling a story of increasing wealth and paternalistic concern. The intimate, cellular nature of Manningham's

Figure 65 (above, left)
St Paul's Church, built in 1847 at the heart of Manningham village.
[DP071738]

Figure 66 (above, right)
St John's Wesleyan Methodist Chapel was built in 1879 at a cost of £14,634 and originally contained 1,000 seats. There is a large Sunday school to its rear.
[DP071624]

Figure 67 (above)
St Luke's Church was built in 1880 and was paid for by general public subscription. At the time it was considered imperative by the church authorities that a new church was built to serve the spiritual needs of the large population around Manningham Mills.
[DP071626]

Figure 68 (above, right)
St Cuthbert's Church, Wilmer Road, was designed by W H and J H Martin and opened in 1890–2. The Catholic mission originally started for Irish workers at Manningham Mills.
[DP065473]

residential web, and the wide social range that it embraced, led to some striking juxtapositions. For example, between Lister Park and Manningham Mills are three places of worship – St John's Chapel (Wesleyan Methodist), St Luke's Church (Anglican), and St Cuthbert's Roman Catholic Church – two of which have substantial adjacent schools. St John's (Fig 66) on Park View Road was built in 1879 in a simple Gothic style, perhaps to challenge the Anglican churches, and was the only Methodist chapel in Manningham to be arranged to accommodate liturgical services. St Luke's (Fig 67), Victor Road, the daughter-church of St Paul's,[10] was consecrated in 1880 to serve the large population located around Manningham Mills and to alleviate overcrowding at St Paul's. For five years prior to this Samuel Cunliffe Lister had allowed the dining room at Manningham Mills to be used for Sunday afternoon services. St Cuthbert's (Fig 68) was built slightly later, in 1890–2, on Wilmer Road. St Cuthbert's mission had begun in 1877 in a building on Beamsley Road for Irish Catholic workers at Manningham Mills and was served by clergy from the earlier-established St Patrick's Church on Westgate. Architecturally unremarkable, St Cuthbert's was notably enriched by the highly sculptural Stations of the Cross carved for the church and installed in the 1920s by the

artist Eric Gill who was converted to Catholicism there (Figs 69 and 70). The presence of three such prominent places of worship in such close proximity, in what was then a new residential area, provides us with an insight into the nature of interdenominational competition at the time and also illustrates the role of such faith buildings as rallying points in an expanding suburban landscape.

Life in Manningham also varied to some extent from class to class and from area to area. A fleeting impression of the villa lifestyle of a wealthy manufacturer with a home in Manningham and a factory in Bradford is afforded by some snippets from the *Leeds Mercury* pertaining to the life of Benjamin Harrison, who lived at Wordsworth Cottage (long since demolished) on Oak Lane and died in 1866, aged 53. Harrison was a worsted manufacturer (successor to J G Horsfall at the North Wing works on Brook Street) and also a Justice of the Peace. In December 1857 the *Mercury* reported that a fire had broken out in his children's nursery following their building of what the paper described as a 'figure or edifice on the floor, with several chairs and books and paper' while playing in the afternoon. The alarm was raised when the servants heard the sound of breaking glass and, because Mr Harrison was not at home at the time, his groom, with the help of a 'Mr Redman', extinguished the fire with buckets of water although not before the furniture and several valuable

Figure 69
The interior of St Cuthbert's Church, Wilmer Road.
[DP065471]

Figure 70
One of the Stations of the Cross in St Cuthbert's Church, Manningham, which were designed and carved by Eric Gill who was converted to Catholicism there. Gill also executed the sculptures of Joseph and Mary and St Anthony which stand in the nave.
[DP065487]

Figure 71
No. 4 Mount Royd (right), the childhood home of poet Humbert Wolfe, author of Now a Stranger.
[DP071827]

pictures and other property had been destroyed.[11] Harrison was perhaps staying in or near Hellifield when the fire broke out because, as the *Mercury* recorded in 1863, he owned 1,500 acres (607ha) of enclosed grouse-shooting land containing wood, meadow and pasture.[12]

For the middle and lower-middle classes at a somewhat later period two memoirs exist to shed invaluable light on the varieties of day-to-day experience, conveying a strong sense of separate worlds which only occasionally overlapped. Manningham was the childhood home of the poet Humbert Wolfe (1885–1940), the Italian-born son of Martin Wolfe, a German-Jewish worsted and woollen merchant and immigrant to Bradford. Humbert Wolfe's childhood experiences are vividly recorded in an autobiographical account of his early years entitled *Now a Stranger*, published in 1933. Wolfe's family lived at No. 4 Mount Royd (Fig 71), just off Manningham Lane, during

Figure 72
The upper front garden at No. 4 Mount Royd which,
Humbert Wolfe lamented, was 'for some reason not to be
used for cricket'.
[DP071826]

the 1890s. Their neighbours included two doctors, including Dr Adolf Bronner who, as Wolfe recalls, set off from Mount Royd to his consulting room on Manor Row at nine o'clock every morning in a well-appointed cab. There was also a militia colonel, a solicitor and a textile-shipping merchant. They evidently formed a fairly close-knit community who all knew one another, even though their professional and business worlds were different, meeting for card games one evening a week in one of their houses and jointly governing the use of the communal front gardens (Fig 72).

The genteel seclusion of Mount Royd is highlighted by the terms in which Wolfe describes nearby Manningham Lane. He paints a picture of the street as a bustling, raucous place with steam trams (like a railway train consisting of a carriage pulled by an engine) but notes how 'an isolating wall fended off Mount Royd, its carriage drive and its great hollow from the roaring neighbourhood of the Lane'.[13] He also describes the way in which Siegfried Pinner, the shipping merchant, would drive himself '… like a small ship's figurehead through the waves of Manningham Lane on his way to his warehouse',[14] and how, while Mr Pinner worked, Mrs Pinner would leave to place orders with the greengrocers and butchers of Darley Street, one of Bradford's main shopping streets, in the morning and spend the afternoon at ease, sitting in the first-floor drawing room of their home at Mount Royd.

Wolfe draws a further contrast between the private gated community of Mount Royd and Parkfield Road, which had no bar and was public, enabling anyone who wished to tramp down it. Parkfield Road (Fig 73) led to Manningham Station which has long since closed and been removed, but Wolfe recalls it as an unremarkable wayside station 'between two sharp hills'.[15] On the Mount Royd side, rows of Victorian villas with gardens ran down to meet it while on the other side were straggling desolate fields and a quarry – a vivid image of the railway and valley bottom as a boundary between two worlds. The station was an exceptional place for Wolfe as a boy because it was the only place where a breach was made in the continuity of everyday life. It was from here that his family caught the trains that took him on day excursions to the countryside and on holidays to the seaside. Otherwise his world centred on Mount Royd whether he was attending school, spending his leisure time bowling a hoop in Lister Park with children his own age, playing illicit games of cricket on the Mount Royd lawns or stealing wood from his

Figure 73
Parkfield Road formerly ran from Manningham Lane to
Midland Road and connected the Lane with
Manningham Station.
[DP071833]

neighbours for bonfire fuel. One of the main themes that arises from Wolfe's memoirs is just how German his world and the wider neighbourhood were and how normal this seemed to everyone. J B Priestley, writing in the 1930s about pre-First World War Bradford, reinforces this view when recalling how the German-Jews 'were so much a part of the place when I was a boy that it never occurred to me ask why they were there'. Even though 'Bradford was determinedly Yorkshire and provincial', he observed, '… some of its suburbs reached as far as Frankfurt and Leipzig'.[16]

A near-contemporary of Humbert Wolfe in Manningham was Kathleen Binns, the daughter of an English worsted merchant. She lived as a child from 1900 in a bay-fronted through-house (not a back-to-back) on Athol Road (Fig 74). Even she recalled how her first school, a little private establishment off Oak Lane, was run by a German lady who began each day's lessons by making her class recite the Lord's Prayer in German. At the age of 86 Kathleen Binns wrote an account of her childhood called *A Family Affair: My Bradford childhood, 1900–1911*, and in it she recalls her life, and that of her family, during the Edwardian period. Her father was a hard-headed businessman and a commercial traveller in the family textile business, Geo Binns & Co, which was in its third generation of family management and kept a warehouse in the town. He travelled extensively, but the rest of the family mostly stayed put in Manningham. For the children, Kathleen and her sister, life was otherwise very circumscribed and they were not encouraged to play with strangers – 'Life came to us rather than our venturing out to seek it … like … a German band marching along the road',[17] while their mother seemed to be permanently occupied by household tasks as the family was not able (or willing) to employ servants. According to Kathleen Binns the family and social circles were entirely centred on Athol Road, with the exception of her grandparents who lived in relative grandeur (able to employ a live-in maid) in a house in the

Figure 74
Athol Road, the street on which Kathleen Binns, author of
A Family Affair: My Bradford childhood 1900–1911, lived.
[DP071807]

gated St Mary's Terrace (Fig 75). For Kathleen's family Manningham was
entirely self-sufficient domestically and they did not need to visit the shops in
town because everything they required could be purchased in Oak Lane. Mrs
Binns's life must have been quite different from Mrs Pinner's at Mount Royd,
even though their husbands were seemingly in a similar line of business. Just
as for Humbert Wolfe, however, Lister Park was the children's playground and
for Kathleen it was a 'paradise', but one she primarily enjoyed with her sister
and grandfather. It was only on Sundays, when the family went to a Quaker
Meeting in Fountain Street, that the two sisters regularly did anything with
both their mother and father. In contrast Wolfe recalls how it was on Sundays
that the young men and women of the German-Jewish community would

Figure 75
St Mary's Terrace, home of the grandparents of
Kathleen Binns.
[DP071840]

promenade in Lister Park, the women typically exchanging views on household matters, the men solemnly discussing the price of mohair. Despite the proximity of their homes and the common trade that their fathers followed, religion, nationality, class, gender and age almost certainly conspired to keep them largely apart. Their vivid accounts of childhood in Manningham during the 1890s and 1900s offer insights into just two of the many different worlds that co-existed in Manningham at the time.

A mosaic

Manningham in the second half of the 19th century was a complicated place. It was home to the factory owners but also to those who worked their mules and looms and all levels of the merchant classes – all tiers of professional life and every variety of tradesmen were represented. Some were Bradford born and had migrated from the town to the suburbs in search of better housing and, perhaps, new jobs. Others were migrants from further afield – other West Riding towns and villages or from other parts of Yorkshire, from more distant parts of the country including London and Scotland, and of course Germany and other parts of Europe. Whatever their origins they became part of Manningham and their children Manningham's own. Each had their own territory, however, even if they seemed to rub shoulders with one another. The wealthiest lived insular lives with their servants, in clusters of what were almost closed communities in private streets such as Clifton Villas or, on a smaller scale Devonshire Terrace, or in gated terraces or rows of semi-detached villas beside Manningham Lane such as Blenheim Mount and Mount Royd which had their own carriage drives and shared but exclusive gardens. Others lived in open streets but even then often grouped in micro-communities of four households, dictated by the design of tunnel back-to-back houses and the shared facilities that these entailed. Each territory was the product of a development mechanism designed to provide suburban housing for its inhabitants, whether through the operation of a building society, co-operative society, freehold land society, private speculation or factory provision. In its way Manningham was as multicultural at the end of the 19th century as it would be at the beginning of the 21st.

4

New cultures

At the turn of the 20th century Bradford was riding high on the crest of a century of economic success. Its importance had been recognised in 1897 when the town was elevated to the status of a city, and by 1900 the boundaries had been expanded such that Bradford now included Thornbury, Heaton, Allerton, Bolton, North Bierley, Thornton, Idle, Eccleshill and Tong (Fig 76). Manningham meanwhile was a suburb in its prime – wealthy, stylish, exclusive yet cosmopolitan in parts, but socially mixed. It was the product of a century of rapid change, urban expansion and technological progress. Manningham had been shaped by the human needs of an industrialising city which had reached out and engulfed the small hamlet at the heart of an outlying township, creating in the process one of its most affluent residential districts. As such it was fitting that the proud city's crowning glory, the Edmund Cartwright Memorial Hall (Fig 77), opened in 1904, should be located there. Paid for by Samuel Lister (now raised to the peerage as 1st Baron Masham), and built on the site of his old home in Lister Park for the benefit of the whole city, it was designed by the distinguished partnership of Simpson and Allen (also the architects of Glasgow's slightly earlier Kelvingrove Art Gallery). Henceforth

Figure 76 (right)
Ordnance Survey map of Manningham published in 1909.

Figure 77 (left)
The Edmund Cartwright Memorial Hall stands on the site of Manningham Hall, the former home of the Lister family. Samuel Cunliffe Lister paid for the building which was designed by the London-based architectural partnership of Simpson and Allen. [DP032913]

Manningham Mills and Lister Park epitomised the marriage of industry and art which symbolised a modern city that had reached maturity.

In May 1904 the Hall and Lister Park were the focal point of the City of Bradford Exhibition, an exuberant celebration of the city's self-confidence and new-found status. The Bradford Exhibition of 1904, which ran for six months, was on a scale without precedent in the city and the event was opened by the Prince and Princess of Wales as part of a two-day visit to Bradford which also included the unveiling of Alfred Drury's statue of Queen Victoria in Victoria Square, and a private visit to Manningham Mills. The Exhibition involved the construction of a number of substantial temporary buildings in Lister Park, of which virtually no trace survives today, including an Industrial Hall a little to the north of Cartwright Hall, a relocated Somali village, and a concert hall along with bandstands and entrance gatehouses.

The pomp and self-congratulatory nature of the Bradford Exhibition reflected the city's pride in its achievements, self-confidence and optimism for the future. This optimistic mood, however, was oblivious to the fact that the world was changing. Few could have foreseen that as the 20th century unfolded Bradford and Manningham would be faced by new challenges that would radically alter Bradford's trade, and even the composition of its people, several times as populations ebbed and flowed, driven by the global economy of which Bradford had made itself such a part. Even before the Bradford Exhibition, the city had received a new wave of foreign settlers fleeing from the pogroms in Russia. It was for them that a new Orthodox Jewish synagogue (Fig 78) was built, in 1905, at Spring Gardens. A decade or so later many of Bradford's most successful merchants who had chosen the pleasant suburb of Manningham as their home and who were either German or of German origin, successors to those who had built fine houses for themselves at Clifton Villas and Oak Avenue and been substantial subscribers to the suburb's charitable institutions and religious buildings, simply left as the First World War erupted and anti-German feeling in Britain ran high. Those who remained changed their names and melted into obscurity. During the years leading up to the war Bradford's trade, especially its export side, had fallen into a slow decline as Continental manufacturers began to catch up and even overtake Bradford in both technology and output of worsted fabrics. The coming of war, however, temporarily halted this decline and provided the conditions for a mini boom.

Figure 78
The Orthodox synagogue on Springfield Place was built in 1905 for Orthodox Jews who came to Bradford to escape persecution in Russia. It is now in use as a mosque following the move of the Orthodox Jewish community to Shipley.
[DP071554]

Many of the English firms that remained in Bradford enjoyed a period of renewed prosperity and confidence during the war and immediately after it – notoriously so and to such an extent that the poet T S Eliot, when looking to express the essence of unwarranted self-assurance in *The Waste Land* (1922), sneeringly likened it to 'a silk hat on a Bradford millionaire'.[18] The boom ended soon after the war but lasted just long enough to create a false sense of security about the future which perhaps left many ill-prepared for what was to follow.

In the early 1920s Bradford's export trade dwindled dramatically. As demand for the city's products fell so did prices and profits, and traders began to go out of business. The biggest losers were the middle men – the merchants who had made their money not by manufacturing or by shipping but by finding customers, buying from the manufacturers and selling on. Many of them lived in Manningham, in the fine villas and grander terraces like Apsley Crescent and St Paul's Terrace. By the late 1920s Bradford was in the grip of the nationwide recession and by the 1930s most of the leading merchant firms had folded. As J B Priestley observed in the early 1930s: 'Not only have all the big merchanting houses disappeared but a great many of the English firms too. Wool merchants, whose names seemed to us like the Bank of England. Not one or two of them, but dozens of them.' He also painted a vivid picture of the business world the 'middle men' had inhabited, describing them as 'gentry' who spent their hours 'lounging, in the cafes playing dominoes or chess … with the maximum of freedom and the minimum of responsibility. The air was fragrant with the Latakia and old Virginia in their pipes. But not now. The fairy tale of trade has been rudely concluded. Those swarms of genial smoky parasites have gone.'[19]

The Bradford of the 1930s was a very different place from the city that had exhibited itself so proudly and celebrated its ties with empire and the world in 1904. Its character was more provincial, less cosmopolitan, than it had been for nearly a century. Even so textile manufacturing continued, although the structure of the industry changed, and an already strong engineering industry continued to grow. Failing family businesses were taken over, firms merged and processes were amalgamated in single concerns. Many manufacturers ceased making cloth altogether and switched instead to yarn production. By the end of the decade, however, the worst of the slump was over and orders for Bradford's manufacturers began to pick up. The Second World War meant hefty orders from the government for khaki battle dress to clothe the troops, albeit under tight government regulation.

With the ending of hostilities came the removal of government control and a return to free trade although by now the industry lacked an adequate workforce. Even as early as 1935 this problem had been recognised – boys wanted more security than the mills could offer, for girls the prospect of a job as a weaver lacked glamour. Immediately after the war a large number of Italians and eastern Europeans arrived, the latter mainly from Poland and Ukraine but also from Lithuania, Estonia and Hungary. Many wished to escape the grip of the Soviet Union. Some were former Polish servicemen who had fought with the Allies, some were from displaced persons' camps in liberated Germany, and some were former prisoners of war. Keen to maintain the traditions and cultures of the countries they had left, especially those occupied by the Soviet Union, the settlers established cultural, religious and social clubs. For this the large villas of Manningham were ideal and both the Latvian and Estonian communities, for example, established clubs in former residences at Clifton Villas (Fig 79 and *see* Fig 26), while a Hungarian cultural and social centre was established at Walmer Villas. Similarly the new Ukrainian community converted the former St John's Wesleyan Methodist Chapel on Park

Figure 79
The Latvian Club of Bradford at No. 5 Clifton Villas.
[DP071536]

View Road for use as a Ukrainian Catholic church. The new incomers readily found employment in the textile factories, especially in the wool-combing branch where working conditions were particularly unpleasant and the labour shortage most acute. The experiences of two Polish sisters, Helen and Olga, who contributed to *Tales and Trails of Manningham* (the DVD that accompanies this book) are probably fairly typical. Their whole family arrived in Britain in 1948 and lived at first on an army camp in Scotland but moved to Bradford in 1955, drawn mainly by the jobs on offer. They lived at Grosvenor Terrace where they enjoyed the bustle and neighbourliness generated by the 16 families who lived there at the time. Their father worked first in a foundry and then in a carpet mill. One of the sisters also worked for 22 years as a weaver in a mill, although the other found such employment intolerable due to the noisiness of the factory environment. The sisters' younger siblings went to school at Belle Vue and in time went on to universities, found work elsewhere and left Bradford, leaving their two sisters who now share a house on Birr Road alone.

In the later 1940s people began to arrive from the West Indies, lured by the promise of work, and from 1951 onwards Indians, Pakistanis and Bangladeshis followed suit. They lived at first in back-to-back houses and working-class terraces in and around Lumb Lane, and were employed in the textile factories and also as bus crews. The fresh injection of willing labour was followed by a number of technical innovations and diversification, notably into carpet manufacture. In the 1950s smoke stopped pouring from factory chimneys in Bradford for the first time in a century and a half as large steam engines powering a whole mill were replaced by small electric motors, one for each machine. But in spite of all, the trend for Bradford manufacturers was one of contraction and ultimately of closure. Lister's business at Manningham Mills decreased dramatically in the 1980s before closure early the following decade. The year 1990 was considered to be one of the worst years for the Bradford textile industry in living memory, and the decade that followed witnessed a succession of mill closures which broke its back.

For Manningham this meant the end of its industrial sector. The factories are, for the most part, still there, but most, like Illingworth's Whetley Mills, Brick Lane Mills (now a burnt-out shell) and Drummond's Lumb Lane Mills, are empty and awaiting new uses. In contrast, the old residential districts remain full of people, the majority of them from various parts of Pakistan and also from Bangladesh – and the predominant religion is Islam. They had come originally seeking employment in the textile industry and had worked in the now-redundant mills. When closure came, a number chose to leave, relocating to Birmingham and London in search of fresh opportunities, but a larger number stayed, determined to build new lives and worlds and create new opportunities for themselves and their children. They did so because Bradford was home and they were fond of it, as Khadam Hussain (another contributor to the DVD) who came to Manningham in 1963 and stayed puts it: 'Bradford is the best city in the world and England is the best country in the world … Manningham is the best place in Bradford.'

Memories of life in the mills and the collective sadness that was felt when Manningham Mills, especially, closed are now fading. A new generation no longer looks back to the days when textile manufacturing was all-important to Bradford's economy. That is part of history. When the factories ceased to provide employment many of those who had stayed at first found work as bus and taxi drivers. In time, however, Manningham moved on and new and successful careers were established as carpet wholesalers, food wholesalers, shopkeepers and property dealers, often in re-used historic buildings. The shops on Carlisle Road and Oak Lane are trading successfully, although Manningham Lane has yet to regain its former primacy. Mosques have replaced redundant Nonconformist chapels and Sunday schools and at the beginning of the 21st century faith is once again at the core of community identities. Manningham now has many mosques. The first were established in existing buildings, originally intended for different purposes, such as the former St Luke's Sunday School on Victor Street, but now there are fine purpose-built structures (Fig 80). Mughal gardens have been built in a rejuvenated Lister Park, which is once again a favourite place for people of all ages and creeds and a showpiece for family visitors from overseas. Manningham's historic buildings, especially the large, solid and well-built houses, are especially cherished and appreciated. The more substantial terraces and semi-detached villas make ideal homes for large south-Asian families. Community networks remain close-knit, and although car ownership has risen steeply in recent years, Manningham is still a place where many journeys are undertaken on foot, and where many needs such as worship and shopping are typically met locally.

If the dominant cultural identities of Manningham have changed dramatically since the Second World War, some aspects of life there have altered perhaps less than we imagine since the Victorian era. Manningham is no more a single place now than it was during its Victorian heyday. Now, as then, it is a rich mosaic of worlds that make up a district which is unified by the outstanding quality of its architecture and building materials and which is still very much fit for purpose after a century and a half of change. As the DVD that accompanies this book demonstrates, there is a real feeling of optimism and pride in the area among its communities.

Figure 80
Jamia Masjid Hanfia Bradford on the corner of Carlisle Road and Ambler Street.
[DP071813]

5

Conservation and change

There is a growing recognition that renewal and regeneration need not mean sweeping away all that remains of the past. While quality of life is about jobs, services and housing, it is also about the environment. It is about creating places where people want to live, work and visit and about keeping those which are valued and evoke special memories. People increasingly understand that the historic environment has a key part to play in holding on to a sense of identity and local distinctiveness. The special character of individual places is more and more seen as an asset. Conservation, therefore, lies at the heart of the renewal process, accommodating and welcoming change but managing it so that historic buildings, places and landscapes are retained and revitalised (Fig 81).

Bradford deserves to be recognised as one of the great stone cities of England, bearing comparison with that better known architectural gem, Bath. The quality of its honey-coloured Pennine sandstone buildings, liberated from industrial grime by the stone cleaning of the 1970s and 1980s, is second to none. It has iconic buildings such as the imposing Victorian Gothic City Hall, the classically detailed St George's Hall, the wonderful Wool Exchange inspired by the palaces of Venice and, of course, Lister Mills (Fig 82), as Manningham Mills is now known, with its landmark chimney.

Figure 81
Hanover Square. Several years ago English Heritage funded the conservation and restoration of a number of properties in Manningham under the Manningham Conservation Area Partnership scheme. One of the most impressive projects was to restore a group of houses in Hanover Square. Many were in very poor condition, some were derelict, but now they are home to a thriving community, mainly of Pashto and Hindko-speaking people from the Bhatan region of north-west Pakistan, and have been for 20 years or so. Properties here rarely come up for sale, changing hands through family connections.
[DP071590]

Figure 82
Bradford, and especially Manningham, is fortunate in possessing landscapes, views and historic buildings of high quality which must provide the inspiration for change.
[DP071786]

We learn from this book that Manningham has undergone waves of progressive change over the last 200 years and it continues to be a living, working and changing place that is rich in history, high-quality historic buildings and landscapes. The casual visitor is constantly surprised by the variety and richness seen in both wide-ranging and intimate views. A journey though the area reveals the complexity of this close-knit historic environment – terraced and back-to-back houses with a backdrop of mills; the glimpse of a church spire or, nowadays, a minaret; the grandeur of a public building, chapel or synagogue; groups of attractive houses in informal squares; hidden gems like the Old Manor House (Fig 83) and the Bradford Tradesmen's Homes.

The traditional appearance of the Old Manor House and the cottages of textile outworkers remind us of Manningham's early history, before it became part of a great city. The later buildings, which mark Bradford's expansion in the 19th century, speak of the confidence and affluence of those times through the quality of their construction and their adaptation of bold national styles. These buildings give the area its special character.

Lister Mills is an extraordinary statement of industrial ambition, but other textile complexes, including Whetley Mills, Lumb Lane Mills and Brick Lane Mills, although plainer in style, express their function powerfully and define their localities. The same quality and craftsmanship is to be found in Manningham's smaller buildings, ranging from the villas of the wealthy industrialists and merchants to the terraces and back-to-backs lived in by the thousands of workers who helped to make the city prosperous. The smooth ashlar stone of some of the best terraces, the carved details, the durability and quality of the building materials all lift Manningham out of the ordinary. Even the humble back-to-backs were substantially built and were well above the housing standards in many contemporary cities.

While some buildings and streets may be regarded as commonplace, closer consideration reveals their value as the well-built, well-detailed and well-loved background to the everyday life of many generations of Bradfordians (Fig 84). The rows of shops, the public buildings such as the Free Library on Carlisle Road and the police station on Church Street, the open spaces, particularly Lister Park, and the places of entertainment and leisure, including pubs and cinemas, all played a part in the life of the community. Even apparently quite ordinary-looking areas have unique stories to tell. Girlington, we now know,

Figure 83
It is important that any conservation and refurbishment scheme is based on a detailed understanding of the building so that significant features that tell its story can be safeguarded. Here we see a sample being taken from an early timber at the Old Manor House, Rosebery Road, so that it can be accurately dated using dendrochronology (tree-ring dating) to help with understanding the age and development of this important early house. Putting together a successful scheme to restore this building and give it a sustainable future must be a priority for action.
[DP071433]

represents an important experiment in democracy and everywhere the influence of the co-operative movement is evident in the blocks of houses built by building societies and building clubs.

Bustling Carlisle Road was once home to an up-market toyshop that restrung tennis racquets and a high-class china shop. Its busy shops now offer colourful Asian textiles and halal meat, as well as a variety of fruit and vegetables beyond the dreams of Victorian shoppers (Fig 85). But it continues to serve the day-to-day life of the community, it is thought of as home, and it is these everyday aspects of the urban landscape which give Manningham, and on a wider scale the lively cosmopolitan city that is Bradford, its own unique identity.

It is now nearly 10 years since the City of Bradford Metropolitan District Council launched its 2020 Vision for the long term regeneration of the District, and in 2004 the Council and Yorkshire Forward commissioned a masterplan for Manningham to show how the 2020 Vision would be focussed there. The

Figure 84
The entrance porch at Oak Well, Oak Lane.
[DP071830]

Figure 85
Carlisle Road is still a busy shopping street, as it was over 100 years ago, but many properties have lost their historic details and their special character is being threatened. To help people make positive changes to their properties Bradford Council has published detailed design guidance to encourage sympathetic reinstatement and improvement.
[DP071816]

aim of the *Manningham Masterplan*[20] is to provide a strategic framework for regeneration and to identify significant projects, working with buildings, sites and people, which will provide the means for change for the better. Manningham has a range of excellent resources that can contribute to its rejuvenation including delightful Lister Park, the splendid Lister Mills, Bradford City Football Ground, the busy Carlisle Business Centre, and local people who are enthusiastic about their future in Manningham. The *Masterplan* aims to celebrate and build on the positive aspects of Manningham, acknowledging its heritage while identifying key projects to tackle the physical, social, economic and environmental challenges it faces. We hope that this publication will assist in the delivery of the *Masterplan* by encouraging better public understanding of the value of the area's heritage and ideas on how to manage it.

There is no doubt that change is needed and that it must take a variety of forms. Opportunities must be taken to encourage more diverse employment, while social facilities require investment. Regeneration of the historic environment, of Manningham's buildings, streets and open spaces is part of this process. Care and attention given to degraded buildings and streets can make a huge difference to the quality of people's lives and to the prospects for inward investment.

The last decade has witnessed two very large projects that have contributed significantly to the renewal of the area. People are now, once again, justifiably proud of their beautiful Park and the stunning Cartwright Hall. Exciting new children's play areas, restoration of the picturesque lake, and the facelift given to the botanical gardens mean that Lister Park (Fig 86) is once again the focus for many community activities and enjoyed by people of all ages. It is a vital resource for schools in the Bradford area, the bandstand has become a well-liked venue for concerts, the boating lake is once again a popular place to visit and the new Mughal Garden (Fig 87) has become a destination in its own right. The icing on the cake was when 'lions' returned to the Park in 2009 following a campaign by the Friends of Lister Park to reinstate the much-loved sculptures which had been missing for many years. All in all Lister Park is a wonderful example of the potential that historic parks in our towns and cities have to become a focus for community pride and bringing people together.

Figure 86 (above)
The renovation of Lister Park is nationally recognised as an outstanding restoration scheme. It is especially valued by the many people who can once again enjoy the beautiful park at the heart of their community. The historic designed landscapes in our towns and cities have a major part to play in the regeneration process as, by creating a focus for community pride and a peaceful haven away from the hustle and bustle of the city, they enrich and add quality to our lives.
[DP071777]

Figure 87 (right)
Historic landscapes are not static. They evolve and change over time as trees mature and fashions in planting change. The decision to introduce the Mughal Garden, a totally new element, into Lister Park was a bold one, but it is a decision that has paid off. The quality of the design and its associations with local people's cultural background means that the garden has meaning and importance within the community. It is a resounding success and people are justifiably proud of it.
[DP032915]

Figure 88
The future of Lister Mills has been a major concern since the 1970s, and when velvet production finally stopped in the 1990s it seemed to be the final nail in the coffin for the complex. It was the creative vision of Urban Splash that secured a future for the Mills, but difficult decisions had to be made along the way. The new penthouses are not to everyone's taste but this unconventional adaptation has added a new dimension to the former Velvet Mill and to the city's skyline, marking the regeneration of the area. They are a fine example of how high-quality new design can complement an historic building. [DP071068]

Lister Mills, an enormous statement of Victorian enterprise and pride, had suffered for many years before silk velvet production finally ended in the 1990s. A chance viewing prompted Tom Bloxham, of innovative developers Urban Splash, to enquire about the mills and Urban Splash eventually purchased them in 2000. Phase one of their redevelopment saw the conversion of the Silk Warehouse into 131 contemporary apartments, commercial space for Manningham Mills Community Centre and a performing arts studio, Mind the Gap. Begun in 2003, and completed in 2006, this imaginative and inspirational scheme has inaugurated a new future for the redundant mill buildings while simultaneously creating a new resource to serve the wider community. A second phase of work, on the Velvet Mill, is well underway and includes the introduction of dramatic new curved penthouse apartments which rise above the parapets of the old spinning mill – a fine example of how high-quality new design can complement historic buildings and signal new life (Fig 88). It is also a hearts-and-minds exercise. This massive project has required significant investment and represents a major commitment to Manningham itself, raising aspirations for the wider area and reinforcing the belief that there is a long-term sustainable future for Manningham as a community.

Regeneration is, however, about much more than 'flagship' projects such as Lister Mills and Lister Park. It must touch the area as a whole and must seek different ways of achieving its goals. The provision of good housing lies at the heart of a successful community. In any programme of regeneration, it is now recognised that success will not come from the uncaring clearance of rows and rows of terraced houses that characterised housing renewal in the 1960s, or from a rigid belief that nothing must change. The way forward lies in policies that build upon local people's ambitions for a better standard of living within their existing, well-loved and established communities. We have found out that people in Manningham care passionately about their historic buildings. The variety of housing in Manningham is a great resource, people enjoy living there and it meets their needs well. The area has never suffered from the problems which prompted the Government to embark on its Housing Market Renewal Initiative: demand for houses is high, very few houses are vacant, and the area is not depopulated. Continuing to use and adapt existing houses is the sustainable way to provide places for people to live. Refurbishment is

Figure 89
Sometimes arriving at a new use for a building requires
compromises to be made. Greenfield Chapel, Carlisle
Road, has been adapted by putting in a false ceiling
between the galleries and removing the possibly
dangerous plasterwork of the original ceiling. It is no
longer possible to appreciate the full volume of the space
in all its splendour, but by retaining the gallery pews the
history of the building can still be seen and understood.
Sometimes hard decisions have to be made in order to
keep a building in active use.
[DP071720]

economically viable, and historic properties can easily meet modern standards
of energy efficiency without harming their appearance and character. For
instance it is straightforward to draught-proof traditional wooden sash
windows and this, together with lined curtains, shutters or blinds can often
achieve the energy efficiency standards sought for new buildings.

Of more concern is what the future holds for the historic public buildings
in Manningham. They are at crisis point for many reasons. Some religious
communities have dwindled or moved away (Fig 89), there have been changes
in health and social care provision and people now use their leisure time in
different ways (Figs 90 and 91). As well as being fine examples of architecture
and craftsmanship, these buildings play an important part in helping us to
understand the day-to-day life of the community and how society has changed
over the years. Without adaptation to new uses, many of them will be
condemned to a slow and sad decline. Redundant buildings such as the
Bradford Children's Hospital (Fig 92), St Catherine's Home, the Bradford
Synagogue (Reform) on Bowland Street and the former police station on

Figure 90
The Mowbray Hotel. The recent downturn in the licensing trade means that a number of public houses have gone out of business. Also under pressure are the clubs and hotels that have taken over some of the larger villa properties. It may be time to consider a change of use for these buildings.
[DP071733]

Figure 91
Buildings such as the former Marlboro cinema add interest and variety to places as well as holding a special place in many people's memories. This building may have found a new future as an event and wedding venue and adaptive reuse to meet new community needs brings benefits for both the building and the people who use it.
[DP071630]

Figure 92
Changes in the National Health Service mean that St Catherine's Home and Bradford Children's Hospital (shown here) which once served the whole city are now redundant. While they remain empty they are at risk of decay. Conversion to residential use may be the way forward.
[DP065446]

Church Street (Fig 93) all need to attract new investment and embrace change, adding a new chapter to their story.

These buildings, together with the former mill complexes (Fig 94), must be a priority for creative thought, conservation effort and investment. Changes may need to be made and what is particularly important is that alterations are informed by an understanding of each building and what makes it special, so that they work with, rather than against, its particular qualities. It is necessary to balance the impact of change against the need to achieve long-term sustainability and wider social benefits for the community. In times of limited resources, a key priority is to secure the future of those buildings which are of most value. Successful schemes, such as the use of the substantial former church hall on Victor Street by the Jamia Mosque (Fig 95), give historic buildings a viable long-term future and make it possible for them to be valued by a new generation of users.

Successful regeneration requires commitment from all those who have an interest in the area. Central and local government both play a key role in the process. Unlike the rapid developments of the 18th and 19th centuries, the process of change today is regulated by the planning system. This provides the nationwide legislative framework that shapes the way in which decisions about the historic environment are made. 'Listed Buildings' legislation allows us to recognise, protect and regulate changes to individual buildings of 'special architectural or historic interest'. The designation of 'Conservation Areas' allows our local authorities to identify, protect and manage change within 'areas of special architectural or historic interest, the character and appearance of which it is desirable to preserve or enhance'. Parts of Manningham are protected in this way. The City of Bradford Metropolitan District Council's Conservation Team is at the forefront of good conservation practice, having carried out a comprehensive programme of conservation area assessments, appraisals and management plans. The five Manningham conservation areas – Apsley Crescent, Eldon Place, North Park Road, St Paul's and Southfield Square – all have detailed *Conservation Area Assessments* which were reappraised and updated in 2007.

These *Assessments* establish in detail what contributes to each conservation area's character and special interest and describe the changes that have taken place over recent years. They have revealed that, while

Figure 93
Important in the social history of Manningham, the former police station has been replaced by a new building and now stands empty and uncared for. It is one of Manningham's landmark buildings and must be a priority for creative reuse.
[DP065781]

Figure 94
Manningham's redundant textile mill complexes are major landmarks and an important part of the area's history. The conversion of Manningham Mills has demonstrated that new uses can be found for such structures but some factories still lie empty or at best underused.
[DP071841]

Figure 95
Jamia Mosque, Victor Street. The successful reuse of this former Sunday school as a mosque has given it a renewed community purpose. By finding new uses for historic buildings that are relevant to the community today we can help to sustain a sense of identity, continuity and belonging.
[DP071615]

Figure 96
Traditional features, particularly windows and doors, all contribute to the character and quality of our historic buildings and areas. Because of the amount of materials and energy used in building them, the continued use of older properties is the sustainable way to provide housing. By simple measures such as insulating roofs, draught-proofing windows and using condensing boilers to run central heating systems they can often reach the energy efficiency standards achieved by new housing. [DP071811]

Manningham's historic buildings retain many distinctive features and details, the strength of character of the area continues to be under threat from their removal and alteration (Fig 96). Changes to chimneys and the addition of modern-style dormer windows can affect the skyline and the impressive wider views over Manningham (Fig 97). Replacement or removal of boundary walls detracts from views along streets and damages the historic settings of

Figure 97
The addition of modern-style dormers not only affects the appearance of streets but also the skyline and the impressive wider views over Manningham and Bradford. There is particular pressure on smaller properties to create extra bedrooms for larger families.
[DP071789]

buildings (Fig 98). Painting or rendering of stonework and inappropriate mortar, pointing, and stone cleaning can all spoil the overall look of individual properties and of groups of buildings, as well as leading to longer term maintenance problems.

Commercial premises with shop fronts tend to retain fewer traditional features, and modern and inappropriately detailed shop fronts are common and spoil the appearance of some streets. Manningham is unusual in having a substantial number of its historic shop premises still in commercial use and it is important to take opportunities to reinstate traditional features while supporting local businesses.

To raise awareness and understanding and to improve decision making, by both the Council and by individuals, Bradford City Council now has in place a

Figure 98
No. 1 Clifton Villas. The special character of an area does not just come from its buildings, it also depends on the quality of the spaces between them and how they sit in the streetscape. Changes to boundary walls to make parking spaces harms views along streets and creates unattractive surroundings to buildings. In addition, it is now also recognised that because of climate change we need to take steps to reduce the amount of hard surfaces in our towns and cities and use more permeable materials, such as gravel and appropriate planting, to allow storm water to soak away. This will bring benefits – it will help with the flooding problems caused by heavy rain and will greatly improve the visual quality of many of our streets. [DP071531]

detailed set of management proposals for each conservation area. In addition, well-illustrated and easy to understand advice on the repair and maintenance of historic buildings and detailed shop-front design guidance can be easily found on the Council's website, and people have the chance to meet the Council's specialist conservation staff at a monthly conservation area forum. These measures help to ensure that repairs, alterations and development result in appropriate changes that respect the character of the area and keep it special.

The quality of the historic environment in Manningham has already been recognised by investment from a broad range of organisations, including the Heritage Lottery Fund, Yorkshire Forward and developers such as Urban Splash. English Heritage has provided grants towards the repair of Hanover Square, the Bradford Synagogue (Reform) (Fig 99) and Lister Mills. The Heritage Lottery Fund has supported the scheme to restore and improve the facilities in Lister Park, which had been blighted by under-use, vandalism and the perception that it was no longer a safe place to be.

The careful management of Manningham's historic and architectural assets and of its unique environmental qualities will be a key factor in delivering Bradford City Council's aspirations for the wider city (*see* Fig 81). Detailed understanding of Manningham's development has been provided by the research carried out for this book. The vision provided by Bradford City Council in the *Manningham Masterplan* and the *Conservation Area Assessments and Management Proposals* acknowledges the very special qualities of the area and its potential to address the challenges it faces in a positive way.

Always diverse and cosmopolitan, Manningham is a complex area, where there is still a powerful sense of the past, a sense of continuity and a sense of place. It is a suburb of high-quality buildings, spaces, views and details, rich with memories and cultural associations. We firmly believe that everyone values a sense of place and that recognition of how an area has developed, what makes it special, and how we each fit in to that history, enriches our lives.

It has been proved time and time again that the sensitive reuse and adaptation of our historic buildings can form the cornerstone of successful regeneration schemes and it is vital that conservation of the historic environment should be put at the heart of our thinking about development. If it is not, then future generations will be unable to place themselves in

Figure 99
The finely detailed decorative interior of the Bradford Synagogue (Reform), Bowland Street. The dispersed nature of the Reform Jewish community in the Bradford area means that the future of the Bradford Reform Synagogue is uncertain. Every effort needs to be made to support the congregation in developing a sustainable vision for this unusual building.
[AA038929]

history, measure the present against the past, or feel a sense of identity and belonging.

Manningham must remain a vital viable suburb (distinctive in character and appearance and embracing a variety of activities and interests) where significant buildings of the past are retained and adapted alongside high-quality new architecture. To succeed it must reconnect with the city centre, reveal and renew the superb quality of its buildings and spaces and ensure that new development enhances its powerful sense of place.

Notes

1 Fieldhouse 1981, 34
Eligibility for the Poll Tax in 1379 included everyone aged 16 and over with the exception of the poor who nationally accounted for about 40% of the population. It is therefore possible that the actual adult population of Manningham in 1379 might have been in the low 30s.

2 Cudworth 1896, 133

3 Cudworth 1896, 18

4 Fieldhouse 1981, 74

5 Cudworth 1896, 153–4

6 Cudworth 1896, 1

7 The *Yorkshire Observer* of 1836 and Robert Baker quoted in Fieldhouse 1981, 124

8 Engels 1987, 81–2

9 Reach 1974, 17

10 *A Short History of the Church and Parish of St Luke's Manningham on Commemoration of the Jubilee 1930*

11 The *Leeds Mercury*, 5 December 1857

12 The *Leeds Mercury*, 17 January 1863

13 Wolfe 1933, 6

14 Wolfe 1933, 55

15 Wolfe 1933, 3

16 Priestley 1997, 140–1

17 Binns 1988, 4

18 T S Eliot 1922 *The Waste Land* lines 233–4

19 Priestley 1997, 142

20 City of Bradford MDC 2005

References and further reading

Baines, Edward 1822 *History, Directory & Gazetteer of the County of York*. Leeds: Edward Baines

Binns, Kathleen 1988 *A Family Affair: My Bradford childhood, 1900–1911*. Bradford: Bradford Libraries & Information Service

Birdsall, Michael, Szekely, Gina and Walker, Peter 2002 *The Illustrated History of Bradford's Suburbs*. Derby: Breedon Books

City of Bradford Metropolitan District Council 2005 *Manningham Masterplan*

Cudworth, William 1896 *Manningham, Heaton and Allerton*. Bradford: W. Cudworth

Engles, Friedrich 1987 *The Condition of the Working Class in England*. (First pub in Germany in 1845, this translation first pub in the USA in 1886). London: Penguin Classics

Fieldhouse, Joseph 1981 *Bradford*. Bradford: Watmoughs and City of Bradford Metropolitan City Council

Firth, Gary 1997 *A History of Bradford*. Chichester: Philimore

Giles, Colum and Goodall, Ian H 1992 *Yorkshire Textile Mills: The Buildings of the Yorkshire Textile Industry 1770–1930*. London: HMSO

Keighley, Mark 1989 *A Fabric Huge: The story of Listers*. London: James & James

Keighley, Mark 2007 *Wool City*. Bradford: Wool Publishing

King, John Stanley 2001 *Heaton: The best place of all*. Bradford: Bradford Arts, Museums and Libraries

Leach, Peter and Pevsner, Nikolaus 2009 *The Buildings of England: Yorkshire West Riding: Leeds, Bradford and the North*, Newhaven and London: Yale University Press

Priestley, J B 1997 *English Journey*. (First published in 1934, this edition 1997). London: The Folio Society

Reach, Angus Bethune (ed C Aspin) 1974 *The Yorkshire Textile Districts in 1849*. Helmshore: The Blackburn Times Press

Reynolds, Jack 1983 *The Great Paternalist: Titus Salt and the growth of nineteenth-century Bradford*. London: Maurice Temple Smith in association with the University of Bradford

Robertshaw, Wilfrid 1934 'The Township of Manningham in the Seventeenth Century', *The Bradford Antiquary: The Journal of The Bradford Historical and Antiquarian Society* Volume VIII (New Series Volume VI) 1940. Bradford

Sheeran, George 2005 *The Buildings of Bradford: An illustrated architectural history*. Stroud: Tempus

Sheeran, George 2006 *Brass Castles: West Yorkshire new rich and their houses 1800–1914*. Stroud: Tempus

Sheeran, George 1990 *The Victorian Houses of Bradford: An illustrated guide to the city's heritage*. Bradford: Bradford Libraries and Information Service

Wolfe, Humbert 1933 *Now a Stranger*. London: Cassell and Company

Other titles in the Informed Conservation series

Behind the Veneer: The South Shoreditch furniture trade and its buildings.
Joanna Smith and Ray Rogers, 2006. Product code 51204, ISBN 9781873592960

Berwick-upon-Tweed: Three places, two nations, one town.
Adam Menuge with Catherine Dewar, 2009. Product code 51471, ISBN 9781848020290

The Birmingham Jewellery Quarter: An introduction and guide.
John Cattell and Bob Hawkins, 2000. Product code 50205, ISBN 9781850747772

Bridport and West Bay: The buildings of the flax and hemp industry.
Mike Williams, 2006. Product code 51167, ISBN 9781873592861

Building a Better Society: Liverpool's historic institutional buildings.
Colum Giles, 2008. Product code 51332, ISBN 9781873592908

Built on Commerce: Liverpool's central business district.
Joseph Sharples and John Stonard, 2008. Product code 51331, ISBN 9781905624348

Built to Last? The buildings of the Northamptonshire boot and shoe industry.
Kathryn A Morrison with Ann Bond, 2004. Product code 50921, ISBN 9781873592793

England's Schools: History, architecture and adaptation.
Elain Harwood, 2010. Product code 51476, ISBN 9781848020313

Gateshead: Architecture in a changing English urban landscape.
Simon Taylor and David Lovie, 2004. Product code 52000, ISBN 9781873592762

Manchester's Northern Quarter.
Simon Taylor and Julian Holder, 2008. Product code 50946, ISBN 9781873592847

Manchester: The warehouse legacy – An introduction and guide.
Simon Taylor, Malcolm Cooper and P S Barnwell, 2002. Product code 50668, ISBN 9781873592670

Margate's Seaside Heritage.
Nigel Barker, Allan Brodie, Nick Dermott, Lucy Jessop and Gary Winter, 2007. Product code 51335, ISBN 9781905624669

Newcastle's Grainger Town: An urban renaissance.
Fiona Cullen and David Lovie, 2003. Product code 50811, ISBN 9781873592779

'One Great Workshop': The buildings of the Sheffield metal trades.
Nicola Wray, Bob Hawkins and Colum Giles, 2001. Product code 50214, ISBN 9781873592663

Ordinary Landscapes, Special Places: Anfield, Breckfield and the growth of Liverpool's suburbs.
Adam Menuge, 2008. Product code 51343, ISBN 9781873592892

Places of Health and Amusement: Liverpool's historic parks and gardens.
Katy Layton-Jones and Robert Lee, 2008. Product code 51333, ISBN 9781873592915

Religion and Place in Leeds.
John Minnis with Trevor Mitchell, 2007. Product code 51337, ISBN 9781905624485

Religion and Place: Liverpool's historic places of worship.
Sarah Brown and Peter de Figueiredo, 2008. Product code 51334, ISBN 9781873592885

Storehouses of Empire: Liverpool's historic warehouses.
Colum Giles and Bob Hawkins, 2004. Product code 50920, ISBN 9781873592809

Stourport-on-Severn: Pioneer town of the canal age.
Colum Giles, Keith Falconer, Barry Jones and Michael Taylor, 2007. Product code 51290, ISBN 9781905624362

Weymouth's Seaside Heritage.
Allan Brodie, Colin Ellis, David Stuart and Gary Winter, 2008. Product code 51429, ISBN 9781848020085

To order through EH Sales
Tel: 0845 458 9910
Fax: 0845 458 9912
Email: eh@centralbooks.com
Online bookshop: www.english-heritage.org.uk

Manningham today

KEY

1 Hammond Square

2 Garden Terrace

3 BPISL store and houses

4 St Cuthbert's RC Church

5 Back-to-back houses on Wilmer Road

6 St John's Wesleyan Methodist Chapel

7 Edmund Cartwright Memorial Hall

8 Clock House

9 Manningham Mills

10 St Luke's Church

11 Victor Street Mosque

12 Fairmount

13 Lilycroft Road School

14 Bradford Tradesmen's Homes

15 Nos. 36–48 Heaton Road

16 Old Manor House

17 St Catherine's Home

18 Bradford Children's Hospital

19 Nos. 11, 13, 15 Skinner Lane

20 St Paul's Church

21 Blenheim Mount

22 Mount Royd

23 Oak House Estate

24 Bolton Royd

25 Parkfield House

26 Rose Mount Villa

27 Site of Manningham Railway Station

28 Valley Mills

29 Nos. 30–40 Whetley Hill

30 Former police station

31 Southfield Square

32 Apsley Crescent, Walmer Villas, Mornington Villas

33 Clifton House

34 No. 8 Clifton Villas

35 Lumb Lane Mosque

36 The Belle Vue Higher Grade Schools

37 The Belle Vue public house

38 Bradford City Football Club

39 Lumb Lane Mills

40 Bradford Synagogue (Reform), Bowland Street

41 Orthodox Jewish Synagogue

42 Hanover Square

43 Peel Square

44 Brick Lane Mills

45 Whetley Mills

46 Girlington Estate

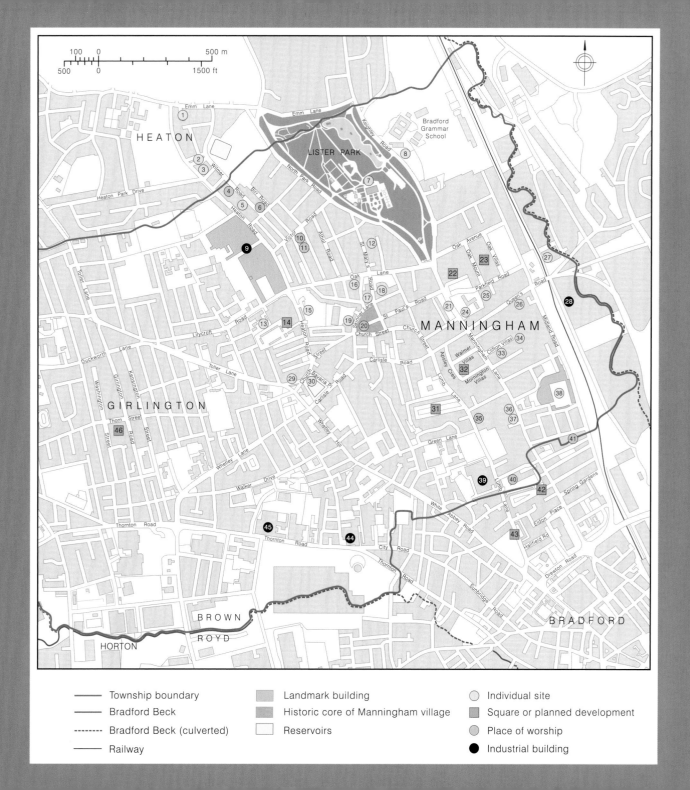

Tales and Trails of Manningham

Tales and Trails of Manningham was produced in 2008 as part of an English Heritage outreach project that ran hand-in-hand with the research undertaken for this publication.

With the help of a local community facilitator, English Heritage worked with a number of people who live in Manningham, providing them with an opportunity to share their views – to have a 'voice' in the research, share their memories and to put forward their own perspectives on the area.

Tales and Trails consists of a series of interviews with residents of different ages and backgrounds. The residents take the viewer on a walk through the suburb where they talk about their memories and how the area has changed, focussing not just on the built environment but also intangible heritage, for example, how textile-rich Manningham used to smell and sound. Other residents offer their thoughts and perceptions on present-day Manningham and how the diverse multicultural community there has embraced the area and made it home.

For further information about English Heritage outreach projects please visit our community projects page at www.english-heritage.org.uk or write to, The Outreach Department, English Heritage, 37 Tanner Row, York, YO1 6WPUK